GOLDEN ZEPHYR

GOLDEN ZEPHYR

Nāgārjuna

A Letter to a Friend
bShes-pa'i spring-yig (*Suhṛllekha*)

Mi-pham 'Jam-dbyangs rnam-rgyal rgya-mtsho

The Garland of White Lotus Flowers:
A Commentary on Nāgārjuna's
"A Letter to a Friend"
bShes-spring gi mchan-'grel padma-dkar-po'i phreng-ba

Translated from the Tibetan and annotated by
Leslie Kawamura

DHARMA PUBLISHING

TIBETAN TRANSLATION SERIES

1. *Calm and Clear*
2. *The Legend of the Great Stupa*
3. *Mind in Buddhist Psychology*
4. *Golden Zephyr* (Nāgārjuna)
5. *Kindly Bent to Ease Us, Parts 1–3*
6. *Elegant Sayings* (Nāgārjuna, Sakya Pandita
7. *The Life and Liberation of Padmasambhava*
8. *Buddha's Lions: Lives of the 84 Siddhas*
9. *The Voice of the Buddha* (Lalitavistara-sūtra)
10. *The Marvelous Companion* (Jātakamālā)
11. *Mother of Knowledge: Enlightenment of Yeshe Tshogyal*
12. *The Dhammapada* (Teachings on 26 Topics)
13. *The Fortunate Aeon* (Bhadrakalpika)
14. *Master of Wisdom* (Nāgārjuna)
15. *Joy for the World* (Candrakīrti)
16. *Samdhinirmocana Sūtra*

Illustrations:
Cover and frontispiece: Nāgārjuna
Page 2: Lama Mi-pham

ISBN: 0–913547–21–6 (pbk)
Library of Congress card number: 75–5259

Typeset in Fototronic Laurel and printed in the
United States of America by Dharma Press

10 9 8 7 6 5 4 3

May the ocean of the Buddha's intention,
through the advice given by the spiritual teachers
Nāgārjuna and Mi-pham,
fulfill all wishes, like a cool mountain breeze.

CONTENTS

Foreword   ix
Introduction   xi
The Garland of White Lotus Flowers: 1
    A Commentary on Nāgārjuna's "A Letter to a
    Friend" by Lama Mi-pham
Appendices
    Lama Mi-pham's Table of Contents   94
    Sa-skya Paṇḍita's Table of Contents   108
    Literature on the *Suhṛllekha*   114
    Tibetan Line Index to Nāgārjuna's *Suhṛllekha*   120
Glossary of Tibetan Terms   137
Bibliography   154
Index   158

FOREWORD

For centuries, beginning Dharma students have traditionally studied "A Letter to a Friend" because it provides a concise and thorough introduction to the entire Buddhist path. By examining the four noble truths and the six perfections, Nāgārjuna and Lama Mi-pham describe, logically and poetically, the internal patterns of experience which lead to the Buddha's enlightenment.

Throughout our lives we are constantly searching for some lasting satisfaction, but too often we are blinded by our own confusion and struggling. If our minds are not balanced, our action will not be balanced. So our dissatisfaction and internal conflict provide the raw material for growth. If we thoroughly understand our own suffering, we can lead ourselves out of much confusion. Then our understanding passes beyond words and beyond philosophy and becomes a living experience.

The Buddha's understanding emerged from his own experience of being human. So the Dharma teaches us first to look at ourselves with complete openness and honesty. Clear and accurate self-observation awakens in us the desire to change unpleasant situations. Whatever situation we are in, try to learn from it rather than escaping or refusing to deal with it. There is really no way we can ultimately escape facing ourselves and taking responsibility for our actions and the quality of our everyday awareness.

Buddhism abounds in advanced philosophical and psychological techniques, but all of these are founded on learning to take care of ourselves properly. This means that we can teach ourselves, we can heal ourselves, we can guide ourselves. The process of proper self-nurturing is like rubbing together two pieces of wood to produce a fire. Once the fire is lit, once we have gained the attentiveness and inner confidence of the Buddha, we can continue to create a positive, balanced attitude and find lasting satisfaction.

The essence of Buddhist teachings can best be understood by internalizing their meaning. The more you study and practice, the more you will understand the teachings through your own experience. So use this text to examine your life carefully. With sincere study and strong determination comes clarity, certainty, and a broad, healthy point of view. The more you test these teachings in your daily life, the more you will *become* that understanding—not just for one day, but moment to moment, in each situation.

Founder, Nyingma Institute   TARTHANG TULKU RINPOCHE
Berkeley, California

INTRODUCTION

Golden Zephyr, the full title of which is *The Garland of White Lotus Flowers: A Commentary on Nāgārjuna's "A Letter to a Friend,"*[1] is a commentary by the nineteenth-century Nyingma lama, Mi-pham, on Nāgārjuna's much-quoted verse text, the *Suhṛllekha*. Although these two authors lived nearly eighteen centuries apart, there is a freshness and lucidity in these texts that disguise their relative antiquity, for they are as practical and relevant as though they had been composed just yesterday. If any work exhibits truly classic dimensions, then it should resist the rust of time and remain universally applicable to the life of each human being. The enduring insight and conciseness of Nāgārjuna's fundamental presentation of the Buddhist path thus prompted Lama Mi-pham to paraphrase and expand the original text for the edification of his own students. So here we have two texts—one built upon the foundation of the other—which offer us the rare privilege of sitting at the feet of two time-honored masters of the Buddhadharma.

---

[1] The Tibetan title of Mi-pham's work is *bShes-spring gi mchan-'grel padma-dkar-po'i phreng-ba*. See Appendix, "Literature on the *Suhṛllekha*."

Nāgārjuna, known in Tibetan as Klu-sgrub, was one of the most subtle dialecticians of all time. He lived during the first half of the second century[2] and was the first teacher to enunciate publicly the teachings of Śūnyatā through his development of the Mādhyamika philosophy. The Mādhyamika movement systematically destroyed two erroneous views of Nirvāṇa —the extremes of nihilism and eternalism. The avoidance of these two extremes—which became known as the 'Middle Path'—crystallized as the underlying tenet of the enormous canonical work of Northern Buddhism, the *Prajñāpāramitā*. Nāgārjuna was most concerned with the nature of reality. He carefully examined man's situation in the world and pointed out how attached we become to our interpretations and analyses of it. With penetrating logic, he investigated the delicate juxtaposition of opposites and pointed out the illusory nature of the world in which we live. The purpose of Nāgārjuna's dialectic was to destroy all preconceived opinions and habitual ways of 'seeing' and to reduce all relative beliefs to a position of absurdity. Nāgārjuna's position is thus 'no position', "for even the most precise analysis and explanation still reflects the human mind's conditioning and obscures its own depth and clarity."[3] His 'middle way', which neither affirms nor denies, thus attempts to sever the paradox of duality in straightforward and practical language.

Nāgārjuna was born in Southern India to a Brahmin family. At an early age he traveled north to Nālanda, the famous seat of

---

[2] The dates of Nāgārjuna have not been established. He seems to have been active just around the turn of the first century of the Christian era. He is considered to be the founder of the Mādhyamika school and is known for many great works on the Mādhyamika, of which the *Mādhyamika Kārikā* is the most prominent. For a discussion on his date and place of birth, *see* P. S. Sastri, "Nāgārjuna and Āryadeva," *The Indian Historical Quarterly*, vol. 31, no. 3, and Richard Robinson, *Early Mādhyamika in India and China*. That Nāgārjuna would appear in the world had been predicted in the *Laṅkā-vatārasūtra* (*Sagathakam*, 165), ed. by Nanjio (Kyoto: Otani University Press, 1956).

[3] For an informal account of Nāgārjuna's philosophy, *see* Tarthang Tulku, "Shunyata," *Crystal Mirror*, 1975, *4*, 171–77.

Buddhist learning. There, under the guidance of Saraha,[4] he was ordained and given the name Śrīmān.[5] One day, Śrīmān encountered a monk named Śaṁkara (bDe-byed), a renowned logician who refuted anyone who chanced to dispute with him. During the discussions which ensued, two small children happened to be listening, and after Śrīmān's victory the children disappeared into the earth. On their invitation, Śrīmān followed and entered the region of the Nāgas (serpent kings). There he gave a discourse on the Dharma and received the *Śatasāhasrīkaprajñāpāramitāsūtra*.[6] He was henceforth called Nāgārjuna.

According to tradition, Śākyamuni Buddha taught to man the exoteric doctrines, teaching at the same time a deeper doctrine which was first preserved by the Nāgas and then brought to earth by Nāgārjuna. His name thus means, 'he who has secured power (*arjuna*) from the Nāgas'. Nāgārjuna became celebrated as one of the 'four suns of the world',[7] is counted as the sixteenth of the eighty-four Mahāsiddhas,[8] and 'the supreme leader of the six ornaments of India'.[9]

The Mādhyamika philosophy also profoundly influenced the theoretical development of Tibetan Buddhism, for the noble Bodhisattva, Śāntarakṣita, introduced Nāgārjuna's teachings during the period of Khri-srong lde'u-btsan's reign (755–97) when Buddhism was formally recognized in Tibet. Following the famous debate (792–94) at bSam-yas Monastery, in which those following the Indian tradition of Buddhism and favoring the gradual approach to Enlightenment gained sway, Khri-srong lde'u-btsan proclaimed, "As concerns theory, let everyone adopt the system of Nāgārjuna." From that time on, it may be said that the early philosophical tradition of the Bud-

---

[4] H. V. Guenther, *The Royal Song of Saraha*, p. 5.
[5] E. Obermiller, *History of Buddhism by Bu-ston*, II, 123.
[6] Ibid., II, 124.
[7] The others are: Aśvaghoṣa, Kumāralabdha, and Āryadeva.
[8] A. Chattopadhyaya, *Tāranātha's History of Buddhism in India*, p. 383.
[9] The 'six ornaments of India' are: Nāgārjuna, Āryadeva, Asaṅga, Vasubandhu, Dignāga, and Dharmakīrti.

dhadharma in Tibet received its inspiration through the spiritual lineage of Nāgārjuna.

According to some traditions, Nāgārjuna is said to have worked in the world for three hundred years and to have lived for another three hundred years in meditative retreat. And according to others, he is still incarnate, for, having learned to transmute his physical body at will into the radiant light of pure being, or 'rainbow body' (*'ja-lus*), he continues to inspire and preserve the essential message of the Buddha's teaching in succeeding generations of followers.

The Nyingma lama, Mi-pham 'Jam-dbyangs rnam-rgyal rgya-mtsho ('the completely victorious ocean of gentle voice', 1846–1912), was a major contributor to the intellectual movement that stimulated a scholastic and practice-oriented 'revival' throughout all of Tibet during the nineteenth and early-twentieth centuries. Mi-pham was born in Golok (East Tibet), where, at the age of twelve, he joined the Me-hor gSang-sngags-chos-gling Monastery of Zhe-chen. There, according to tradition, he spent eighteen months in the hermitage of 'Ju Nyung in tantric propitiation of Mañjuśrī, who favored him with a remarkable vision.

Many of Mi-pham's teachers were considered to be shining beacons in the nineteenth-century cultural renaissance which became known as the Eclectic Movement (*ris-med*) in Eastern Tibet (sDe-dge in Kham), and included dPal-sprul Rinpoche (b. 1807), 'Jam-dbyangs mkhyen-brtse'i dbang-po (1820–92), Kong-sprul blo-gros mtha-'yas (1813–99), rDzogs-chen mkhan-po padma-rdo-rje, and others.[10]

A most versatile and comprehensive scholar, Mi-pham systematized the Sūtras and philosophical Tantras and wrote over thirty-two volumes, including works on music, painting, poetics, sculpture, engineering, chemistry, alchemy, logic, philosophy, tantra, and astrology, as well as two volumes on the

---

[10] *See* Gene Smith, Introduction to *A Commentary on the Bodhicaryāvatāra* by 'Jam mgon Mi-pham rgya-mtsho in *Ngagyur Nyingmay Sungrab.*

Kālacakra Tantra. He was also a creative physician, and his medical works are highly regarded to this day. Unreservedly one of the most imaginative minds to appear in the Tibetan tradition, Mi-pham wrote many brilliant and strikingly original commentaries on important Indian śastras, including Śāntideva's *Bodhicaryāvatāra*, and compiled a dictionary of Tibetan and Sanskrit equivalents for the philosophical and psychological concepts of rDzogs-chen. He was also responsible for collating and editing several oral accounts of the Gesar epic. Manuscripts and blockprints of many other extraordinary treatises by Mi-pham were known to be scattered throughout monasteries in Eastern Tibet.

Inspired by the entirety of the Nyingma lineage, Mi-pham's works reveal a close relationship between philosophy and practice. He compiled and practiced over 200 sadhanas, and at one time spent seven years in meditative retreat. A revered teacher, he traveled throughout Tibet, visiting Ka-thog, rDzogs-chen, and Zhe-chen monasteries many times. While his scholarship is based on a thorough study of previous Nyingma lamas, such as kLong-chen-pa (1308–64) and 'Jigs-med-gling-pa (1729/30–98), his outstanding contribution to the development of Buddhism in Tibet was his method of scientifically systematizing and interpreting Buddhist philosophy into a coherent path.

In *The Garland of White Lotus Flowers*, Mi-pham has ingeniously expanded the 123 verses which comprise Nāgārjuna's "A Letter to a Friend" into a comprehensive preliminary text for his students that they might benefit from the early Buddhist tradition and use these teachings as a source and a guide in their beginning studies.

Nāgārjuna's "Letter" was originally written to a close friend, a king named bDe-spyod, instructing and encouraging him to practice the Dharma in his daily life. From beginning to end, Nāgārjuna appeals to the king's common sense in analyzing the human situation and its attendant frustration. Saṁsāra, he says, simply means being frustrated, and frustrations are produced from insatiable desires.

Nāgārjuna's discussion is one of gentle persuasion and unrelenting logical organization. He extols the preciousness of the human body while emphasizing its fragility and impermanence, and encourages the king to reflect on the certainty of death, which may come at any moment. Human beings are unhappy because they are frustrated, are impermanent in that this moment may be their last, are without an 'independent essence', and are physically impure. Thus, Nāgārjuna advises, "Be mindful." As the Buddha has stated, "Carefulness is the basis of immortality, negligence is the state of death."

According to Nāgārjuna, the Buddhist path begins appropriately, for each of us, in the present situation in which we find ourselves. The human body, which is rare and difficult to obtain, is thus the essential starting point for developing an 'enlightenment attitude'. Therefore, the Buddha said, "Attentiveness to the body is the only path to walk, for it makes sentient beings pure and able to pass beyond frustration and unhappy experiences."

In the Buddhist world-view, all forms of existence—including the gods, demigods, spirits, animals, and hell-beings—are subjected to impermanence which is a constant source of frustration. But the value of suffering is that it may become the catalyst for change. So repeatedly and poetically, Nāgārjuna attempts to startle the king into changing his life style: "If you commit even small offensive acts and do not desist instantly, as with a single sword-like blow, then, when the long night of death arrives, you will come face to face with whatever frustrating effects are produced by your offensive and evil acts."

But no matter how solid and reliable human existence may appear, it is essentially transient. Even a beautiful sunset may point out to us the fleetingness of the moment. So what is truly valuable in this life? Nāgārjuna replies, "Among all possessions, contentment is the best and most excellent treasure. Even if you have no possessions, always be content. . . . Since possessions are fleeting and impermament, and cannot steady the mind or adequately satisfy one's desires, learn to give generously and unreservedly from the heart." Thus the king is instructed to overcome the 'eight worldly concerns'—gain and loss, pleasure and pain, kind and abusive words, praise and blame—and to reject actions which offer little contentment.

Throughout his "Letter," Nāgārjuna provides the king with the essence of the Buddha's teachings by supplying him with a series of carefully selected and concisely defined 'word-lists'. For example, faultlessness, open-mindedness, mental clarity, and purity are the basis of ethical behavior, while the following are dangerous enemies: "Avarice is an overconcern with the material things in life; dishonesty is the intent to conceal one's shortcomings; and deceit is to display an outward appearance of possessing virtuous qualities (even when one does not have them). . . . "

Liberation from suffering, Nāgārjuna finally says, depends on oneself. If one does not rely on oneself, who can be a protector, guide, and friend? "So first intensify your awareness by listening to and learning about the Buddha's teachings, and then, while persisting in ethical behavior, practice meditative concentration through which the mind becomes lucid. Know that frustration is essential to the path of liberation, remove its cause, become involved in actively implementing the removal of any further causes, make the path your very own, and apply yourself to the four noble truths."

Thus we may see that Nāgārjuna's advice is always straightforward, logically precise, and eminently practical. By putting into practice the four noble truths, we may begin to experience the 'truth of the path' and the meaning of our life in this world when the mind has entered—through 'inner calm' and a 'wide perspective'—the state of equanimity. Since "the mind is the root of life's meaning, learn to control your mind."

Nāgārjuna progressively develops in his "Letter" the inner understanding that preceded and accompanied the Buddha's own enlightenment, for "when frustrations and their causes are completely extinguished, there is freedom. The 'path' by which freedom is attained is the noble eightfold path"—the series of instructions into which the Buddha condensed his experience of complete liberation.

These are just a few of the many points which Nāgārjuna makes in his "Letter." By training oneself to see the human situation clearly and by making a detailed investigation of one's own mind, we may learn for ourselves the "precious and profound treasure of the Buddha's teachings, which are like a powerful wish-fulfilling gem." The essence, then, of Nāgārjuna's message may be summarized as follows:

> Awaken, my friend, from your slumber in a routine and
> worldly life—
> It is only a source of frustration!
> Strive continuously for a life of heightened awareness,
> Because it alone is the only source of bliss!

It is this central view and guidance that Mi-pham repeats and expands in his commentary, teaching us how to bring about that which harmonizes with our highest ideals and how to exert ourselves mentally—to look, observe, and see reality 'as it is' through the eyes of an enlightened attitude. In his commentary, Mi-pham thus interweaves an explanation of the 'five Buddhist paths' and encourages his students to practice the six perfections, the last two of which—meditative concentration and discriminating awareness—comprise more than half of the book.

According to Mi-pham, the 'five paths' refer to a continual unfolding of our inner potential. The path begins with an honest and clear observation of our life situation and the 'accumulation' of all that is necessary for our intellectual and spiritual growth. This 'new knowledge' expands our horizons and results in a 'fresh perspective' in which previous obstacles to our growth and happiness disappear. This 'new vision' allows us to see—more clearly than ever before—the intrinsic nature of the universe and our own involvement and relationship to the world. As we grow in this understanding, we give 'life' to this new perspective through our action by living in accord with our inner vision until we begin to perceive everything that constitutes this world as being harmoniously interrelated.[11]

The basic assumption of the five paths—and the six transcending actions or 'perfections' that accompany them—is that we must first 'set out' in order to reach our journey's end. Once we begin to experience for ourselves this 'new vision' and our eyes are opened, past confusions and doubts, and everything that has been obstructing us, fall away and are replaced by the spontaneous arising of a deep and satisfying 'joy'. Thus Mi-pham says, "Have confidence in the Dharma and take to heart these instructions, for they have the power to lead you away from frustration and teach you the root of life's meaning."

Mi-pham, in making his commentary, outlined the text into its various topics and compiled a table of contents (*see* Appendix). The numbering system employed in Mi-pham's Table of Contents, as well as in Mi-pham's prose commentary, should enable the reader to follow the logical progression developed in Nāgārjuna's verse text. The chart appended to the Table of Contents should also be consulted when reading this translation, for it outlines at a glance Mi-pham's analysis and division of the text on the basis of the five paths and the six perfections. Sa-skya Paṇḍita's Table of Contents follows a different enumeration and has also been included for comparison (*see* Appendix, "Literature on the *Suhṛllekha*").

For those wishing to use these texts in conjunction with their study of the Tibetan language, I have included a "Glossary of Tibetan Terms." And for those who may wish to make quick reference to Nāgārjuna's Tibetan verses, which are quoted liberally in various texts, I have also compiled a "Tibetan Line Index to Nāgārjuna's *Suhṛllekha*."

---

[11] For a more complete discussion of the five paths, *see* H. V. Guenther & L. S. Kawamura, *Mind in Buddhist Psychology*, pp. xvi–xxiii, and H. V. Guenther, *Kindly Bent to Ease Us*, pp. 241–44.

This work could not have reached its completion without the unselfish efforts of my teacher, Dr. Herbert V. Guenther, who has spent many laborious hours helping me to read this and other Tibetan texts. Words cannot express my gratitude to him. I would also like to express my appreciation to Mr. Lobsang Lhalungpa, who compared the English translation with the Tibetan and provided many useful suggestions, and to Dr. Keith Scott, who read through the translation for clarity. Without the aid of these *kalyāṇamitras,* this translation could not have reached its present form.

I wish to extend my appreciation, as well, to Tarthang Tulku Rinpoche, Head Lama of the Tibetan Nyingma Meditation Center and the Nyingma Institute in Berkeley, for his keen interest in this translation and his generosity in interpreting difficult passages, and to Dharma Publishing and Dharma Press, for their thoroughness in correcting the manuscript and for their personal care in undertaking this publication.

THE GARLAND OF WHITE LOTUS FLOWERS

A commentary on Nāgārjuna's
"A LETTER TO A FRIEND"

by
Lama Mi-pham

THE GARLAND OF
WHITE LOTUS FLOWERS

Oṁ Svasti

May I be protected by the Roaring Lion—the guru
Mañjuśrīnātha—
Who, with the sword-like blazing luster of appreciative
discrimination,
Has torn out the creepers of the all-pervading darkness
And has bestowed the light of knowledge which consists
of two kinds of awareness.[1]

I rejoice in spreading the Lama's word,
This *Garland of White Lotus Flowers*—[being] a
Commentary on *A Letter to a Friend*, which was
originally well-expounded
By Nāgārjuna, the exalted master and scholar of
commentaries,
In the exact way that the vast and deep teaching of the
Buddha was intended.

Now, the explanation of this text—called *A Letter to a
Friend*, written by Ācārya Nāgārjuna—has the following four
sections:

---

[1]"Two kinds of awareness' refers to an awareness before the formulation of
a concept (*ji-lta-ba mkhyen-pa*) and an awareness which enriches what is
observed by seeing it in its field characteristic (*ji-snyed-pa mkhyen-pa*). See
H. V. Guenther, *The Jewel Ornament of Liberation*, p. 258.

I. Title
II. Translator's homage
III. The body of the commentary ⟨3⟩
IV. Postscript

I. TITLE

In Sanskrit, *Suhṛllekha* ("A Letter to a Friend").

In Tibetan, *bShes-pa'i spring-yig* ("A Letter to a Friend").

A 'friend' refers to [Nāgārjuna's] very close friend, a king by the name of bDe-spyod.[2] A 'letter' is something one sends to another whom one cannot meet face to face.

II. TRANSLATOR'S HOMAGE

Homage to Mañjuśrī, who had been a prince.[3]

The above statement is the translator's homage. [The meaning is] Homage to Mañjuśrī, who is gentle because he has overcome all discomforting afflictions and who is eternally

---

[2] It is difficult to determine who is designated by the name bDe-spyod. There is no doubt that he was a Śātavāhana king. Venkata Ramanan says he was named "Gautamīputra Śatakarṇī who ruled in A.D. 106–30 or, according to another view, A.D 80–104" (*see* A. Chattopadhyaya, *Tāranātha's History of Buddhism in India*, pp. 385–87). Richard Robinson claims that "[Nāgārjuna's] 'Friendly Letter' is dedicated to one of the Śātavāhana (Āndhra) kings, possibly Yajñaśrī" (*see* R. Robinson, *Early Mādhyamika in India and China*, p. 24). Jaideva Singh says, "One of his minor works, *Suhṛllekha* ('Friendly Epistle') is said to have been addressed to the Āndhra king, Śātavāhana. Śātavāhana is, however, regarded not as the name of a particular king, but as the name of a family of Āndhra kings founded by Simuka. Some scholars maintain that Suhṛllekha was addressed to Kaniska" (*see* Th. Stcherbatsky, *The Conception of Buddhist Nirvana*, p. 5). Tāranātha gives 'bDe-byed', but this is a mistake (*see* A. Schiefner's Tibetan text, *Tāranātha de Doctrinae Buddhica in India Propagatione*, p. 57). In H. Wenzel's translation of Nāgārjuna's text into German, the title reads 'König Udayana'.

[3] The full title in Sanskrit is *Mañjuśrī Kumārabhūta*, which is often translated 'Mañjuśrī the Youth'. This misses the associations the Tibetans have of the Bodhisattva Mañjuśrī who, as King Amba, vowed to become a Bodhisattva. *See* H. V. Guenther, *The Jewel Ornament of Liberation*, p. 8, n. 1.

youthful because his being, radiant with the splendor of the two qualities,[4] never grows old.

III. THE BODY OF THE COMMENTARY

This comprises three topics:[5]

    A. Introduction: How [this instruction] is positive in the beginning [§1–4].

    B. Content: How [this instruction] is positive in the middle [§5–170].

    C. Summary: How [this instruction] is positive in the end [§171–176].

A. INTRODUCTION: HOW [THIS INSTRUCTION] IS POSITIVE IN THE BEGINNING

This consists of two parts:

    1. The exhortation to listen so as to make a start.

    2. The advice to listen because it is a means for overcoming contempt.

1 *The exhortation to listen so as to make a start.*

> *Oh, one worthy of the virtues which are naturally wholesome,*
> *In order that you may desire the treasure which comes from*
> *The instructions expounded by the Sugata,[6] I have composed*
> *A short treatise containing Sublime Words worthy of your audience.[7]* [1]

---

[4] *don-gnyis.* 'Two qualities' refer to 'benefiting oneself and benefiting others'. See Mi-pham's *dKon-mchog-gsum,* fol. 5a.

[5] Here reference is made to the Buddha's teaching which is good in the beginning, good in the middle, and good in the end. This reference to the Dharma is found in *Saṁyutta Nikaya,* IV, 314–16.

[6] 'Sugata' is one of many names given to a Buddha.

[7] This and the following italicized verses of Nāgārjuna are not included in Mi-pham's text, but have been added for convenience. The numerals in the

Oh, one worthy of listening to the Supreme Doctrine
whose excellent virtues are naturally ⟨4⟩ wholesome, in order
that you may desire the invaluable treasure which comes from
the very precious baskets of instructions[8] expounded by the
Sugata's voice possessing sixty modulations,[9] I have composed a
short treatise containing those Sublime Words worthy of your
audience.

2 *The advice to listen because it is a means for
overcoming contempt.*

This has two parts:
        3. Laying aside one's contempt for the form in
           which the advice is written,
        4. Laying aside one's contempt for its content.

3 *Laying aside one's contempt for the form in
which the advice is written.*

**Just as the wise ones will respect a statue of the
   Sugata,
Even though it be made of wood [and] however
   [unadorned] it may be,
So in the same manner, although this composition of
   mine may be pitiful,
May you not criticize it, for it is based on the Sublime
   Teaching.** [2]

---

left margin—1, 2, 3, etc.—correspond to Mi-pham's Table of Contents. Numerals in brackets [2] refer to Nāgārjuna's stanzas; numerals in diagonals ⟨4⟩
indicate the beginning of a new folio in Mi-pham's text. The text is most
clearly read in conjunction with Mi-pham's Table of Contents and the
accompanying chart in the Appendix.
  [8] 'Baskets of instructions' refer to the Sūtra (Buddha's sermons), Vinaya
(rules of discipline), and Abhidharma (training of one's cognitive capacity).
See H. V. Guenther & L. S. Kawamura, *Mind in Buddhist Psychology*, pp. 45,
46.
  [9] 'Sixty modulations': See *Mvyut.*, XX; *Dīgha Nikāya*, I, ii, 114; *Saṁyutta
Nikāya*, II, 218.

For example, just as the wise ones bow with reverence before a statue of the Sugata, even though it be made of poor-quality wood and no matter how crude in appearance, so too, although this composition of mine may be a pitiful compilation of words, may you not criticize it, for it is based on the wide and deep Sublime Teaching. This is advice that one should accept.

4 *Laying aside one's contempt for its content.*

> *Although you may indeed have impressed into*
>   *your heart*
> *The multitude of the Buddha's words which are*
>   *well-renowned,*
> *Yet, is it not the case that what is made from chalk*
> *Becomes still whiter in the glow of the harvest*
>   *moon?* [3]

Although you may indeed have noticed and impressed previously into your heart the multitude of the Buddha's words which are well-renowned for being positive in the beginning, middle, and end, and for generating confidence which dissipates the evils of the three gateways,[10] yet is it not the case that what is naturally white, such as paint ⟨5⟩ made from chalk, becomes still whiter than before in the glow of the harvest moon? Certainly, it cannot be otherwise!

B. CONTENT: HOW [THIS INSTRUCTION] IS POSITIVE IN THE MIDDLE

This comprises two parts:
>   5. An explanation that confidence [in the Dharma]
>   is at the basis of a path which supports [those who
>   are on the path to] liberation and an existence
>   freed from conflicting emotions.
>   11. The nature of the path.

---

[10] *sgo-gsum.* 'The three gateways' are the three possible 'avenues' of responsiveness—physical, vocal, and mental.

5   *An explanation that confidence [in the Dharma]*
    is at the basis of a path which supports [those
    who are on the path to] liberation and an
    existence freed from conflicting emotions.[11]

This has two parts:
   6. A summary of the six objects of sustained atten-
      tiveness of a Buddha, which are the basis for
      making pure what must be purified,
   7. A detailed exposition of the last three objects of
      sustained attentiveness.

6   *A summary of the six objects of sustained*
    attentiveness of a Buddha, which are the basis
    for making pure what must be purified.

The Buddha who is victorious, the Dharma, and the
   Saṅgha,
Charity, ethical behavior, and the supernatural, are the
   six objects of sustained attentiveness.
May you conduct yourself in the manner of these
   objects of sustained attentiveness
Whose individual values have been expounded
   thoroughly.   **[4]**

The six objects of sustained attentiveness are:
   a. The Buddha who is victorious over the four bound-
      ary situations,[12]
   b. The Teaching,
   c. The Congregation,
   d. Charity,
   e. Ethical behavior,
   f. The supernatural.

---

[11] 'Those who are on the path' refer to men and gods.
[12] *bdud (māra)*. The 'four boundary situations' are: emotions, death, life in a
form of a living being, and over-evaluated ideas. *See* H. V. Guenther, *The
Jewel Ornament of Liberation*, p. 199, n. 11, and *The Royal Song of Saraha*,
pp. 80–84.

May you conduct yourself in the manner of these objects of sustained attentiveness whose individual values have been explained thoroughly as follows:

    a. The Buddha as one who is naturally involved[13] with himself and with others,[14]

    b. The Teaching as the infallibility of the two realities,[15]

    c. The Congregation as those who have gained a state of awareness and who have become free from ignorance,

    d. Charity as the cause of unsurpassed wealth,

    e. Ethical behavior as the foundation of a person's spiritual growth;[16]

    f. The supernatural means one who is a self-witness,[17] or the achievement of special qualities through practicing principles (*chos*) [appropriate to] an elevated existence.[18]

---

[13] See H. V. Guenther, *The Royal Song of Saraha*, p. 76, where he states that 'involvement' (*lhun-grub*) "refers to the revelation of the essence of Being in our own existence."

[14] These two objectives (*don-gnyis*) refer to one's attainment of a higher spiritual level (*rang-don*) whereby one acts in a way which is beneficial to others (*gzhan-don*).

[15] 'Two realities' generally refer to the 'conventional' (*saṁvṛtti*) and the 'ultimate' (*paramārtha*), but in this case, 'two realities' refer to the two last truths of the four noble truths, namely, the truth of the extinction of frustration ('*gog*) and the path to the extinction of frustration (*lam*). See bLo-bzang sbyin-pa's commentary, p. 7 ('*gog lam gyi bden-pa gnyis*).

[16] *yon-tan*, 'spiritual growth': The foundation of spiritual growth is ethical behavior because it controls actions which arise through body, speech, and mind in view of the three divisions in the path of accumulation. See *Grub-mtha'* fol. 205; *Mind in Buddhist Psychology*, p. xviii.

[17] *rang-gi-dpang-po*, a 'self-witness'. For the Tibetans, *dpang-po* carries the flavor of supernatural forces which are 'witnesses' to our mental attitudes. The notion of there being 'private thoughts' is foreign to them. The supernatural as a witnessing process is an ethical force—not a judge, but a wholesome presence. As such, it is the ten wholesome acts (*dge-ba'i chos bcu*). See §8 of the translation.

[18] *mngon-mtho*, 'an elevated existence'. This refers to men, demigods, and gods.

7   *A detailed exposition of the last three objects of
    sustained attentiveness.*

This comprises three parts:
      8. The supernatural,
      9. Charity,
     10. Ethical behavior.

8   *The supernatural.*

**May you always perform the ten positive acts and
      paths,
Which relate to bodily activities, speech, and thought.
Refrain from things like intoxicating drinks and,
Accordingly, enjoy a positive life.**   [5]

The ten are the seven positive acts and the three paths.
May you always have a proper view of things[19] and perform the
positive acts of giving up these three bodily activities:
      a. taking life,⟨6⟩
      b. taking what is not given,
      c. sexual excess;[20]
of giving up these four acts of speech:
      a. lying,
      b. slander,
      c. idle and foolish talk,
      d. harsh talk;
of giving up these three acts of thought:
      a. selfishness,
      b. malice,
      c. wrong views.

---

[19] To have a 'proper view' means to have confidence in the Buddha's
teaching.
[20] 'Sexual excess' means to have sexual intercourse at an inappropriate
time, in an inappropriate place, and under inappropriate conditions. *See*
H. V. Guenther, *The Jewel Ornament of Liberation*, p. 76.

Turn away from things like intoxicating drinks[21] which are not only objectionable in themselves, but which also impair one's capacities. Accordingly, enjoy a positive life which is freed from vindictive feelings towards others and which is freed from mindless acts. He who attains a goal commensurate with [the seven positive acts and the three paths] is said to have attained a supernatural state.

9   *Charity.*

> *Because you know that possessions are fleeting and*
>   *without intrinsic value,*
> *May you, with a proper attitude, make gifts*
> *To monks, Brahmins, and destitute beings.*
> *There is no better friend than this generous act.*   [6]

Because you know that possessions are fleeting, impermanent, and without intrinsic value for steadying the mind, and therefore have no value or capacity to satisfy one's desires, may you, having rid yourself of an incorrect attitude[22] regarding the act of giving, then make, properly and from the heart, a true gift to monks and Brahmins who are worthy recipients, and to destitute beings who roam about in their own frustrations. There is no better friend than this worldly act of generosity.

10   *Ethical behavior.*

> *You must make faultlessness, open-mindedness, mental*
>   *clarity,*
> *And purity the basis of ethical behavior.*
> *Ethical behavior is said to be the support of everything*
>   *valuable,*
> *Just as the earth is to the animate and*
>   *inanimate.*   [7]

---

[21] 'Intoxicating drinks' is not limited to liquor, but includes similar substances which unnaturally alter perception.

[22] An 'incorrect attitude' involves selfish concern or selfish motivation.

You must make four qualities which purify your ethical behavior the basis of your ethical acts. They are:

a. Faultlessness, [because by this quality] one overcomes the fault of hypocrisy, ⟨7⟩

b. Open-mindedness, [because by this quality] one perfects the conditions which aid one in removing hypocrisy, and thus increase prosperity.

c. Mental clarity, [because by this quality one does not confuse] the path leading to calmness with the path leading to worldly concerns.

d. Purity, [because by this quality one purges] emotionally tainted attitudes which are the causes for hypocrisy.

Just as the earth is the foundation for both the animate, like man, and the inanimate, like mountains and houses, ethical behavior is said to be the support of everything valuable, such as an elevated existence and liberation.

11   *The nature of the path.*

This comprises three parts:
12. A summary,
13. A detailed explanation,
167. The joy of taking to heart its significance.

12   *A summary.*

Liberality and generosity, ethics and manners, patience and tolerance, strenuousness and perseverance,
Meditation and concentration, and discernment and appreciation are the immeasurable perfections.
When these blossom forth, one crosses over the vast ocean of life and
Acquires the strength of the Victorious One.   [8]

By being aware of the most appropriate actions,[23] when these blossom forth in one's own existence, one crosses to the other shore and gains the strength of the Victorious One. When the range of
   a. Liberality and generosity,
   b. Ethics and manners,
   c. Patience and tolerance,
   d. Strenuousness and perseverance,
   e. Meditation and concentration, and
   f. Discernment and appreciation
has become immeasurable, one cuts through the three pure motives[24] by appreciative discrimination which is without discursive thought.[25]

13   *A detailed explanation.*

This comprises six topics:
   14. Liberality and generosity,
   15. Ethics and manners,

---

[23] The word *thabs*, usually translated as 'means' is not a means to any egocentric end, but refers to the 'fitness of action' which "signifies the best possible course of action in a particular circumstance because of the knowledge of the actual situation. The unity of fitness of action and intelligence indicates integration which means that the diverse tendencies in an individual have become harmoniously united." *See* H. V. Guenther, *Treasures on the Tibetan Middle Way*, pp. 20–21.

[24] *'khor-gsum.* The 'three pure motives' have been discussed in *MSA*. There are three kinds: a. without discursive thought (*'khor-gsum-du rnam-par mi-rtog-pa, MSA*, XVII, 6, 7); b. with discursive thought (*'khor-gsum-du rnam-par rtog-pa, MSA*, XVI, 31–35); and c. that which is pure (*'khor-gsum yongs-su dag-pa, MSA*, XII, 11; XIII, 29). *See* §174 of translation.

[25] "The goal is appreciative discrimination. If one strives by first making an effort, then contemplating appropriate action, and finally attaining the goal, the mind becomes settled in the holistic experience. When the mind has become calm, appreciative discrimination is born, and by means of appreciative discrimination the mind is freed from conflicting emotions. Since the six perfections foster 'fitness of action' by which one attains the goal and in turn aids others to attain their goals, these perfections are called 'the deep' and 'the profound'." *See* Sthiramati's *Mahāyānasūtrālaṁkārabhāṣya*, P. ed., vol. 109, p. 5, 1.7–2.1.

20. Patience and tolerance,
25. Strenuousness and perseverance,
28. Meditation and concentration, and
68. Discernment and appreciation.

14 *Liberality and generosity.*

Whosoever honors his father and mother will become a
    praiseworthy one,
Possessing the qualities of a Brahmin or a teacher.
In honoring them, he becomes well-renowned and,
Even in the next life, he will be born into a heavenly
    state.   [9]

Whosoever ⟨8⟩ respects and honors his father and mother
will become no different from a praiseworthy one who possesses the qualities of a Brahmin or teacher. Thus, in honoring
them, he becomes well-renowned by possessing the fine quality
of keeping their kindness in mind because he has understood
their actions. Even in the next life, when he takes a different
existence, he will be born into a heavenly state.

15 *Ethics and manners.*

This has four parts:
16. Ethics and manners which must be observed,
17. Elimination of activities which are incompatible
    with ethics and manners,
18. Cultivation of carefulness, which is compatible
    with them.
19. An exposition, by examples, of the benefits of
    carefulness.

16 *Ethics and manners which must be observed.*

Give up hurting, stealing, improper sex, lying,
Intoxicating drinks and obsession with eating
    food at an improper time,

Lustfully enjoying a luxurious bed, and
Singing, excessive dancing, and jewelry.   [10]

When these eight activities [of renunciation],
Which an Arhat guards as an ethical life, become
   identified with you,
The performance of purifying acts grants to both men
   and women
The attractive shape of gods in the world of
   desire.   [11]

Killing others with a weapon or hurting them by slanderous name-calling;[26] stealing, which is to take something not
given; improper sex, which is to commit adultery; and lying—
these are four acts which cannot be committed when one is
cultivating the carefulness which constitutes an ethical life.
One must give up intoxicating drinks and refrain from the
three activities which are [so easily] made into a cult, namely:

   a. obsession with eating food at an improper time, in
      the latter part of the afternoon,
   b. lustfully enjoying a luxurious bed, and
   c. singing songs, over-indulgence in dancing, and the
      wearing of ornamental jewelry.

When these eight activities,[27] which the Arhat guards
naturally as an ethical life, become identified with you, the
so-called 'performance of purifying acts' grants to both men
and women, because they are not born as eunuchs, ⟨9⟩ the
attractive shape of gods in the world of desire.

---

[26] Killing, injuring, and hurting also implies the intention to do so, as well as
inducing one to do away with his life by extolling death in such words as "Oh,
man, what is the good of this sinful, impure and wretched life? Better is death
than life to you." *See* A. C. Banerjee, *Sarvāstivāda Literature*, p. 135.

[27] These eight, together with frequenting pleasure resorts and accepting
gold and silver, make up the ten precepts (*bslab-pa'i gzhi, śikṣapāda*) prescribed for the novice (*dge-tshul, śrāmanera*). Ibid., p. 113.

17   *Elimination of activities which are incompatible
     with ethics and manners.*

**View as your enemies: avarice, dishonesty, deceit,
     attachment,
Arrogance of showing off,[28] cupidity-attachment,[29]
     hatred and
The vanity of your social status and appearance,
Your learning, your youth, and your power.**   [12]

Avarice is an overconcern with the material things in life.
Dishonesty is the intent to conceal one's shortcomings. *Deceit* is
to display an outward appearance of possessing virtuous qualities [even when one does not have them]. *Attachment* means
to be obsessed with oneself, the enjoyments of life, and the
pleasures of sexual intercourse. *Laziness* is not taking the action
of either accepting or rejecting. *Arrogance of showing off* is to
think, "I have achievements," even when one has attained nothing. *Cupidity-attachment* is pleasure with regards to tainted
perceptual objects.[30] *Hatred* is directed towards an unsatisfying object. *Vanity* is a mental inflation that occurs when you

---

[28] 'Arrogance of showing off' is one of seven kinds of arrogance. The others
are: arrogance, excessive arrogance, pride of excessive arrogance, egoism,
arrogance of thinking small, and perverted arrogance. For a fuller discussion,
see Guenther & Kawamura, *Mind in Buddhist Psychology*, pp. 68–72.

[29] *'dod-chags*, 'cupidity-attachment': *'dod* means to desire something in-
tensely, and having got what one has so strongly desired, one finds that one is
somehow stuck with it (*chags*). The two aspects of desiring and the frustration
of not being able to get rid of what has been desired, is the meaning of
'cupidity-attachment'; hence, *'dod-chags* is not a mere passion or attachment.

[30] *zag-bcas-gi yul*, 'tainted perceptual objects'. 'Tainted' (*zag-bcas*) refers to
all aspects of conditioned reality (*'du-ma-byas*) with the exception of the Path.
See Poussin (transl.), *Abhidharmakośa*, I, p. 6; *The Jewel Ornament of Liberation*, pp. 28, 83. *zag-bcas* is anything which seems to have durable qualities
but which in the end become dissatisfying. Hence, whatever pleasure we
experience in life may seem to be something of the utmost concern, but all the
worry we give it will only result in more frustration because it is bound to
break. 'Perceptual objects' (*yul*) refer to the five types of sensory objects
(color-form, sound, odor, taste, touch) and objects of categorical perception.

regard your social status as that of royalty or as that of a Brahmin, your appearance as handsome or beautiful, your learning as superior from having heard many times the teachings of both the Buddhist and non-Buddhist schools, your youth as eternal youth, and your power as influential. View these, which you think belong to you and consequently to which you have become attached because of their enjoyable qualities, as your enemies.

18 *Cultivation of carefulness, which is compatible with them.*

The Buddha has stated, "Carefulness is the basis
of immortality;
Negligence is the state of death."
Therefore, in order for you to increase the wholesome,
Always be concerned and devoted.   [13]

The Buddha has stated that carefulness, which protects the mind from tainted objects by attending to the wholesome, is the basis of immortality which is deathless and beyond frustrations, and that negligence is the state of death which means to roam about in Saṁsāra. A Sūtra states,[31]

Carefulness is the basis of immortality,
And negligence is the state of death.
Carefulness cannot become a state of death.
Negligence is always death.

Therefore, in order for you to increase, more and more, the wholesome, always be devotedly concerned about the wholesome. ⟨10⟩

---

[31] This verse may be found in Chapter VI, v. 4, of *Dam-pa'i chos dran-pa nye-bar bzhag-pa (Sad-dharma-smṛty-upasthāna-sūtra)* in Lin Li-Kouang *Dharma-Samuccaya Compendium de la Loi,* 2ᵉ Partie, VI à XII (Paris: Maisonneuve, 1969), p. 3. Parallel verses also occur in N. P. Chakravarti, ed., *Udanavarga,* IV, 1 (Paris: 1930), p. 37, v. 1; and *Dhammapada,* V, 21.

19   *An exposition, by examples, of the benefits of
     carefulness.*

*Whosoever was negligent previously
But later became attentive and careful,
Shines forth like the moon freed from clouds,
Just like Ānanda, Aṅgulīmāla, Ajātaśatru,
and Udayana.*   [14]

Even a person who has been negligent previously, but
later has become attentive and careful, shines forth like the
moon freed from clouds, just like Ānanda, a cousin [of the
Buddha] who was full of lust; Aṅgulīmāla, who, owing to
the fact that he had been enticed by wicked friends, was beset
by the bewilderment caused by straying into error and murdered 999 people; Ajātaśatru, who, full of hatred because he
had been unable to become the king, plotted with his evil friend
[Devadatta] and murdered his own father;[32] and Udayana who,
out of hatred and blinded by passion, killed his own mother in
order to commit adultery.

By making the teachings, which counteracted these tendencies, the foundation of their life, the first two became Arhats, the third became a Bodhisattva, and the last one, having
become a god, saw the truth.

------

[32] Ānanda, a personal attendant of the Buddha, persuaded the Buddha to
create an order of nuns (*bhikṣuṇī*) by saying that sex could not come in the
way of a person intent on the realization of Nirvāṇa (*see* Ajay Mitra Shastri,
An Outline of Early Buddhism, p. 142). Ānanda was also a witness to the
rehearsal of the five Nikāyas at the first Buddhist Council (*see* Kern, *Manual of
Indian Buddhism*, p. 2). Aṅgulīmāla (or Aṁgulimālaka) was a famous robber
and murderer in Kosala (*see* Kern, p. 37). There seem to be two accounts
concerning Ajātaśatru: 1. that he succeeded in murdering his father as
recounted here, and 2. that he was given the throne by Biṁbasāra (*see* Kern,
p. 39, and Shastri, p. 43). For Udayana, the text reads *bde-byed*, which is
usually *śaṁkara* or *kṣemaṁkara*. In H. V. Guenther, *The Jewel Ornament of
Liberation*, sGam-po-pa provides similar accounts for Aṅgulīmāla, Udayana,
Ānanda or Nanda, and Ajātaśatru (pp. 124–26).

20   *Patience and tolerance.*

This comprises four parts:
      21. The advice to overcome anger, the cause,[33]
      22. The advice to overcome resentment, the out-
          come,
      23. The fact that a specific outcome results from a
          specific state of mind, and
      24. The advice to refrain from harsh words which
          sustain the state of indignation.

21   *The advice to overcome anger, the cause.*

**Because there is nothing as difficult as patient
    acceptance,
You must not allow an opportunity for indignation
    to arise.
The Buddha has proclaimed that, by overcoming
    indignation, you will attain
A state in which you will not return to a previous
    existence.**[34]   **[15]**

Because there is nothing as difficult as patient acceptance, from the first, you must not allow the opportunity for
indignation to arise. The Buddha has proclaimed ⟨11⟩ that by
overcoming indignation, you will gain, as an effect, a state in
which you will not return to a previous existence. It has been
stated,

> O Bhikṣu! By getting rid of indignation, you will witness the
> fact that you will not return to a previous state.

---

[33] The relationship of these four topics are discussed in *Mind in Buddhist
Psychology*, pp. 66–68, and fig. 3, p. 120.
[34] 'Previous existence' refers to the realm of sensuous desires ('*dod-pa'i
khams*).

22   *The advice to overcome resentment, the outcome.*

> **You say, "He has blamed me, talked behind my back,**
> **And ruined me. He has stolen my property."**
> **Quarrels originate from hostility. When you**
> **Overcome hostility, you will sleep peacefully.**   [*16*]

You say, "This enemy has openly blamed me with harsh words, talked behind my back, and has ruined me by making my shortcomings worse. He has stolen my property." Know that quarrels which take the form of fighting and arguing originate from hostility. If you overcome hostility, you will be freed from resentment and will sleep peacefully.

23   *The fact that a specific outcome results from a*
      specific state of mind.

> **Know that the mind is just like a**
> **Painting on water, sand, or stone.**
> **The emotionally tainted mind belongs to the first.**
> **The last and the best is to desire the quest for life's**
>   **meaning.**   [*17*]

Know that the function of the mind is just like a painting on water, sand, or stone—unstable, stable, or very stable. Of these, the emotionally tainted mind belongs to the first category and is like the painting on water. A painting on stone resembles the positive mind, which desires to enter the quest for life's meaning (*chos*), and is the best, as it will not change.

24   *The advice to refrain from harsh words which*
      sustain the state of indignation.

> **The three kinds of speech—enlightened words**
> **Worthy of taking to heart, true words, and false**
>   **words—**

Are like honey, flowers, and excrement.
The Buddha has said that, of these, the last one must
be given up.   [18]

The three kinds of speech—words worthy of taking to heart, because they accord with what was intended by the Buddha; true words, because they state exactly what is meant; and false words, because they do not tally with anything or are spoken out of ignorance—are, accordingly, ⟨12⟩ words which are like honey, flowers, and excrement. The Buddha has said that, of these, the last one must certainly be given up.

25   *Strenuousness and Perseverance.*

This comprises two parts:
26. The sites in which the foundation of strenuousness and perseverance can be found, and
27. The advice to strive assiduously for that which harmonizes with one's intention and that which can be brought about.

26   *The sites in which the foundation of*
strenuousness and perseverance can be found.

There are four kinds of people—
Those who go from light to light,
Those who go from darkness to darkness,
Those who go from light to darkness, and
Those who go from darkness to light.
Be one who belongs to the first of these.   [19]

There are four kinds of people. Those who go from light to light go from one happy state to another happy state. Those who go from darkness to darkness go from one frustration to another frustration. Those who go from light to darkness go from a happy state to a frustrating state. Those who go from darkness to light go from a frustrating state to a happy state. You be one who belongs to the first category, and go from one happy state to another happy state.

27   *The advice to strive assiduously for that which*
      harmonizes with one's intention and that which
      can be brought about.

> **Know that men are like the mango fruit—**
> **Unripe but appearing ripe;**
> **Ripe but appearing unripe;**
> **Unripe and appearing unripe;**
> **Ripe and appearing ripe.**   [20]

Understand that men are like the mango fruit which has a fourfold aspect of being ripe or unripe, internally and externally. Regarding this, there are mangoes which are unripe internally, but appear ripe when seen from the outside. There are those which are ripe internally, but appear unripe when seen from the outside. There are those which are unripe internally, and appear unripe externally. There are those which are ripe internally, and appear ripe externally.

28   *Meditation and concentration.*

This comprises three parts:
      29. Setting out,
      62. Content, ⟨13⟩
      63. What one must do afterwards.

29   *Setting out.*

This has two parts:
      30. The removal of instabilities which are not con-
          ducive to meditation and concentration, and
      61. Adopting the four immeasurable divine states of
          the mind which are conducive to meditation and
          concentration.

30 *The removal of instabilities which are not
    conducive to meditation and concentration.*

> This has four parts:
>> 31. Being transfixed by an object,
>> 40. Being transfixed by the eight worldly concerns,
>> 49. Being transfixed by possessions,
>> 55. Being transfixed by pleasures.

31 *Being transfixed by an object.*

> This has two parts:
>> 32. Controlling the senses so as to control one's ideas,
>> 37. Removing attachments, because one has understood what things are.

32 *Controlling the senses so as to control
    one's ideas.*

> This has four parts:
>> 33. The advice to guard the senses against the desire for another man's wife.
>> 34. The advice to guard the senses against other desires,
>> 35. The confusion which results from not controlling the senses, and
>> 36. Praise of one who is able to control his senses.

33 *The advice to guard the senses against the desire
    for another man's wife.*

> **Do not look at another man's wife, but if you should,
> Think that she is as old as your mother, daughter,
>   or sister.
> If you should become attached to her,
> Think properly that she is nothing more than an
>   accumulation of filth.**   [21]

Do not look at another man's wife purposefully, but if you should [look at her] in the course of things, think that she is as old as your mother who is older than you, a daughter who is younger, or a sister who is the same age. Do not become attached to her, but if you should, think properly that her body is nothing more than an accumulation of filth.

34   *The advice to guard the senses against*
      other desires.

> ***Keep guard against a scattered mind, as you have***
>   ***learned,***
> ***Like a son, a treasure, or your own life.***
> ***Think of the pleasures of cupidity as deadly, [like]***
> ***Poison, pointed weapons, an enemy, and fire.***   **[22]**

In the manner that you have learned, keep guard against a scattered mind, which cannot keep still for even a moment. ⟨14⟩ Keep guard as you keep guard over a son, a treasure, or your own life. When you have learned how to do so, hold on to what you have learned. Pay attention, because if you do not, you will not learn the implication of the word 'transfixed'. You must therefore turn on the lamps[35] which keep the mind steady on the flow of the garlands of words. Know this to be like the following examples:

   a. A mother always watches cautiously over a playful child because she sees pleasure as a fearful abyss.
   b. Out of fear that they may be stolen by thieves, one watches over one's treasures both day and night.
   c. Even if your life is at stake, you guard it because you value your life.

After one has cautioned one's mind by making it alert, what are the dangers against which it must be protected? Consider the pleasures of cupidity as deadly, like a snake, poison, a sharp pointed weapon, an enemy, or a pit of fire.

---

[35] 'Lamps' refer to ethical behavior, charity, and contemplation.

35   *The confusion which results from not controlling*
     the senses.

The Buddha has said, "Attachments produce
unhappy states
And are like the Kimpa fruit.[36] **Shun them!"**
These chains bind one to various
Existences as a prisoner of Saṁsāra.   [23]

What happens when one does not control one's mind?
The Buddha has said, "Attachments are unhappy states and
produce great frustrations. They are like the Kimpa fruit." The
Kimpa fruit, as is said in the *Dran-nye*,[37] "comes from a tree
found in a Western island. If one should eat its fruit in the
morning, he will be dead by the afternoon. Therefore, "Shun
them!" These iron chains bind ⟨15⟩ one helplessly to various
existences as a prisoner of Saṁsāra.

36   *Praise of one who is able to control his senses.*

Know that of those who are victorious over their six
sensory organs,
Which are always unsteady and rove over different
objects, and
Of those who are victorious over their enemies in
battle,
The Wise Ones praise the former as being true
heroes.   [24]

---

[36] *Kimpāka* or *Strychnos nuxvomica*, a kind of cucumber also known as the
fruit of *Trichosanthes palmata* (see Monier-Williams, *A Sanskrit-English Dictionary*, p. 283b). This fruit is native to Ceylon, India, Cochin-China, and
also found in Australia and Indonesia (?). Bucine and strychnine are derived
from it, and a tonic made up of very small quantities of these drugs is used for
muscular disorder. (I thank Prof. H. E. Gruen, Department of Biology, Univ.
of Saskatchewan, for this information.)

[37] *Dran-nye* is short for *Dam-pa'i chos dran-pa nye-bar bzhag-pa* (*Saddharmasmṛtyupasthānasūtra*). This quotation seems to incorporate chap.
VII, v. 31, of the Sūtra and its commentary (Lin Li-Kouang, transl., v. 2, p.
118). 'Kimpa fruit' occurs often as a simile for the effects of *'dod-chags* (cupidity-attachment) in this Sūtra (cf. verses 109, 116, 136, 154, 180). 'Western
island' perhaps refers to Goa and/or Andaman and Nicobar.

Know that of those who are victorious over their six sensory organs, beginning with the eye, whose operations are always unsteady and which continually rove over different objects such as color and form, and of those who are victorious over their enemies in battle, the Wise Ones praise the former kind of men as being true heroes. 'Hero' is used in the sense of steadfastness and does not mean being the object of other people's admiration. To be victorious over enemies in battle is not difficult, but to be victorious over one's mind is one hundred times more difficult because there is not a single person who is not influenced by an object as a result of following his senses when certain tendencies which have been programmed from time immemorial emerge. In short, even animals can be victorious in battle, but to be victorious over the influence of objects is difficult even for a Buddha.

37   ·Removing attachments, because one has
understood what things are.

> This consists of two parts:
> 38. Overcoming attachments by thoroughly under-
> standing a woman's body which is the principle
> pleasure in the world of sensuous desires.
> 39. Removing attachments by knowing how passion
> functions.

38   *Overcoming attachments by thoroughly
understanding a woman's body which is the
principal pleasure.*

> *Seen from a different point of view, the youthful
> Body of a woman is impure, has nine orifices, is like
> A vessel filled with stench and difficult to fill; and
> From another point of view, an adorned covering of
> skin.*[38]   [25]

---

[38] This verse relates the way or method by which one can overcome one's attachment which is a specific internal mental function. The body of a woman

Seen from a different point of view, the youthful body of a woman is impure, has nine orifices, and is like a vessel filled not only with stench, but also with all of the thirty-two ⟨16⟩ things like excreta, urine, and blood; it is difficult to fill no matter how much food and drink one gives. And from another point of view, this vessel of stench is covered with skin and adorned with gold, silver, and silk. Discriminate between the body and its adornments to gain this understanding.[39]

39   *Removing attachments by knowing how passion
     functions.*

*Even if a leper stands near a fire
To assuage the pain caused by worms,
He gains no relief; know that the same
Is true of attachments to passion.*   [26]

A leper stands near a fire to assuage the feeling of pain caused by worms buried under his skin and thereby seems to gain relief when the worms briefly stop crawling. Under these conditions, since the disease is not actually eliminated, the terror of great pain returns once again. In the same way, know that when attachments to passion are not assuaged, they will evermore increase.

---

is used as an example, because a woman's body is one of the sources of strong attachment. In this meditative practice, the image or object of one's desire is examined. For a traditional presentation of this practice, *see* Tarthang Tulku, *Calm and Clear*, pp. 33–41.

[39] It is necessary to overcome attachment by gaining an understanding that, in the final analysis, a body of a woman (or man) is merely a living organism filled with stench. If one does not overcome one's attachment to it, then, because attachment is like salty water, the more one becomes involved with one's attachment, the more one thirsts for it. Although attachments produce pleasurable results at first, attachment is what binds one to Saṁsāra, and, in the long run it can produce only pain. Therefore, the means or method to overcome it is very important.

40   *Being transfixed by the eight worldly concerns.*

This consists of two parts:
    41. Aids to overcoming the eight worldly concerns, and
    44. That which is to be removed.

41   *Aids to overcoming the eight worldly concerns.*

This has two parts:
    42. Aids identified, and
    43. An explanation of those defects and benefits whose presence and absence determine the efficacy of an aid.

42   *Aids identified.*

Make it a habit to think about things
In a proper way so that you will see the absolute.
There is no other practice which can
Confer comparable benefits.   [27]

Make it a habit ⟨17⟩ to think about things in a proper way, just as they are, so that you will see the significance of impermanence, frustrations, the open dimension of reality, and the fact that there is no abiding principle to which a thing can be reduced—all [of these have] the inherent character[40] of the absolute. There is no other practice which has comparable praiseworthy qualities because, internally, one conquers the enemy of the mind through this practice.

43   *An explanation of those defects and benefits*
    whose presence and absence determine the
    efficacy of an aid.

Even if people possess social status, good looks, and
    learning,

---

[40] *gnas-tshul*, 'inherent character', as opposed to *snang-tshul*, 'apparent character'.

*If they are deficient in appreciative discrimination and
    ethical behavior,
They are not worthy of respect. In the same way,
He who has these qualities is praiseworthy even if he
    lacks the other qualities.*   [28]

Even if people possess social status, good looks, and great
learning, if they lack appreciative discrimination, which prop-
perly directs them to a thing, and ethical behavior, which means
to act properly, they are not worthy of respect. In the same
way, a person who thinks properly and has the two qualities
of appreciative discrimination and ethical behavior is praiseworthy even if he lacks other qualities like social status and
so on.

44   *That which is to be removed.*

This consists of two parts:
    45. The eight worldly concerns identified, and
    46. Advice on the removal of the resulting evil.

45   *The eight worldly concerns identified.*

*You who know the world! Gain and loss, pleasure and
    pain,
Kind and abusive words, praise and blame are called
The eight worldly concerns.
Since respectable people do not take them seriously,
    exercise equanimity.*   [29]

You who know the world! Gain and loss of anything you
enjoy; pain and pleasures of your body and mind; kind words
which are pleasant when heard, and abusive words; being
openly praised and secretly blamed—these are the eight worldly concerns because worldly people stay with them, enjoy them,
and cannot go beyond them. ⟨18⟩ Since right-minded and
ethical people do not take them seriously, exercise equanimity
and do not be concerned with them.

46   *Advice on the removal of the resulting evil.*

> This consists of two parts:
>   47. The evil identified, and
>   48. The way to get rid of it.

47   *The evil identified.*

> *May you not do evil even for the sake of a*
> *Brahmin, a priest, a god, a guest, your parents,*
> *Your wife, or your attendants, because*
> *No one else will reap its fruition, hell.*   [30]

May you not do evil—neither for your own sake nor for a
worthy Brahmin, priest, god, a guest who is a friend, your
parents who are your mother and father, nor for your wife or
your attendants. You alone and no one else will experience hell
as its fruition.[41]

48   *The way to get rid of it.*

> *If you commit even small offensive acts and do not*
> *Desist instantly as with a single sword-like blow, then*
> *When the time of death arrives, you will come face*
>   *to face*
> *With whatever effects are produced by your offensive*
>   *acts.*   [31]

If you commit even small offensive acts and do not desist
instantly as with a single sword-like blow, then, when the long
night of death arrives, you will come face to face with whatever
frustrating effects are produced by your offensive and evil acts.
This can be compared with a bird flying in the sky and casting
a shadow.

---

[41] bLo-bzang sbyin-pa's commentary (p. 32) quotes an unidentified Sūtra
which reads: "The results of one's action are not experienced by the earth, the
water, or the rocks. Action has its result in this frail body of man and nowhere
else." A similar quotation can be found in *The Jewel Ornament of Liberation*,
p. 81.

49 *Being transfixed by possessions.*

This has three parts:
    50. A general explanation distinguishing possessions
    to be rejected from those to be accepted,
    51. In particular, rejection of acts which give little
    contentment, and
    52. Aids to rejecting.

50 *A general explanation distinguishing possessions
to be rejected from those to be accepted.*

*Confidence, ethical behavior, charity, learning,
Self-respect which is pure, decorum, and appreciative
    discrimination
Have been declared by the Buddha as the seven
    precious possessions.
Know that the 'benefits' of other possessions are of no
    ultimate value.*   [32]

The active implementation of confidence, ethical behavior, learning, charity, self-respect which is pure and which depends on oneself, decorum which makes others the norm, ⟨19⟩
and appreciative discrimination, has been declared by the
Buddha to constitute the seven precious possessions.[42] Know
that these possessions are of great benefit because they
remove both immediate and long-term[43] impoverishment;
whereas those benefits gained from other kinds of possessions,
while alluring, are unstable, deceptive, and useless for removing the cause which binds one to passion.

---

[42] *'phags-pa'i nor-bdun*, 'the seven precious possessions'. They are said to be
precious because they are free from emotional defilements (*see* bLo-bzang
sbyin-pa's commentary, pp. 33–34).

[43] *mthar-thug*, lit. 'to the extreme', 'ultimate'; here it means 'until one has
achieved liberation'.

51   *In particular, rejection of acts which give little*
     contentment.

   Gambling, seeking out crowds, laziness,
   Relying on evil friends, intoxicating drinks,
   And going out at night are evil ways of living.
   Reject these six which lessen your fame.   [33]

   In particular, such acts as gambling with dice, wandering
about to seek out crowds such as at a bazaar, laziness which
rejects strenuousness, relying on evil friends, taking intoxicating drinks, and going to others' homes at night lead one to
wander about in an evil way of life. Reject these six which
lessen your fame in this life.

52   *Aids to rejecting.*

   This has two parts:
        53. The benefits derived from the aids, and
        54. The evil consequences of not using them.

53   *The benefits derived from the aids.*

   Among all possessions, contentment has been described
   By the Buddha as the best and most excellent.
   Always be contented. If you know contentment,
   Even if you have no possessions, it is a real
        treasure.   [34]

   Among all possessions, contentment has been described
by the Buddha as the best and most excellent because with it
one desires little. Therefore, always be contented. If you know
contentment, even if you have no possessions such as gold, your
experience will be like that of having acquired a real treasure
because the aim of a treasure is to make one content.

54   *The evil consequence of not using them.*

> *Your Majesty! Just as those who own a lot suffer,*
> *Those with little desire do not.*
> *The eminent serpent has as many frustrations*
> *As heads which produce them.*   [35]

⟨20⟩ Your serene Majesty! Just as those who own and hoard a lot of things suffer by losing them, those who have little desire do not suffer in that way. For example, the eminent serpent has as many snake-heads as the number of treasures it owns and has as many innumerable painful headaches as the heads which produce them.

55   *Being transfixed by pleasures.*

> This has three parts:
>   56. Family atmosphere,
>   59. Food,
>   60. Rejection of attachment to sleep.

56   *Family atmosphere.*

> This has two parts:
>   57. That which must be rejected, and
>   58. That which must be accepted.

57   *That which must be rejected.*

> *A wife who, like an executioner, is by nature*
>   *linked with an enemy;*
> *Who, like a queen, annoys her husband;*
> *Who, like a thief, takes even small things—*
> *Reject these three varieties of wife!*   [36]

You must reject three kinds of wife: a wife who, like an executioner, is by nature linked with one's enemy; a wife who, like a queen, annoys her husband; a wife who, like a thief, takes even small things without asking.

58   *That which must be accepted.*

She who is simpatico, like a sister;
She who enters your heart, like a girl friend;
She who wishes to serve, like a mother;
And she who will aid, like a servant—
She must be honored as a family god.[44]   [37]

She who is simpatico, like a sister; she who enters your heart, like a girl friend; she who wishes to serve, like a mother; and she who will aid, like a servant—such a person must be honored like a family god, because she keeps the family together.

59   *Food.*

By knowing that food is like medicine,
May you rely on it without cupidity or avarice.
It is not for power, nor for pride.
It is not for mental inflation, but is only to support
  your body.   [38]

By knowing that food is like medicine, ⟨21⟩ know how to measure it like medicine, in the sense that if you measure more or less than what is prescribed, the medicine will not be of any use. Therefore, the Ācārya [Nāgārjuna] makes a general com-

---

[44] *rigs-gyi-lha*, 'family god.' Nāgārjuna was writing in a Brahmanical society whose religious practices centered around the family and the caste system. Each family paid obeisance to the family gods. A similar practice occurs in Tibetan society, centering on a subclass of worldly gods (*jig-rten-pa'i-lha*) called *pha-mes-gyi-lha*. In times of family misfortune—such as crop failure—Tibetans seek help from such deities. Buddhism has always acknowledged the presence of helping (and hindering) forces and therefore adjusted easily to various folk practices throughout Asia.

ment when he says, "May you rely on it without cupidity or avarice."

A more detailed explanation: The statement, "It is good neither for power nor pride," means that food strengthens the body and is to be eaten for that purpose. Food eaten to gain strength to bend bows is food eaten to nourish one's power. Food eaten to prolong one's youth is food eaten to nourish [the pride one takes in] one's youth. Food eaten as a result of reflecting upon one's looks, health, and youthfulness is food eaten to nourish each of these [preoccupations]. Moreover, when one gains influence as a result of acquiring an attractive appearance through an enrichment in one's diet and thinks, "I cannot help doing these objectionable things like injuring enemies and cohabiting with a woman," this is food for arrogance. Pride as a nutrient is not a nutrient which strengthens one's body, but is food for avarice, because attachment to power, mental inflation, and arrogance cause injury to others. Therefore, food must be eaten only to support your body, which functions so that you may attain a superior reality, which is not involved with such conditions.

60   *Rejection of attachment to sleep.* ⟨22⟩

> *Oh knowledgeable one! During the day and even*
> *during the night,*
> *The time between sunset and sunrise, even while you*
> *are asleep,*
> *Let it not be fruitless!*
> *Do not let sustained attentiveness slip away during*
> *that time.*   [39]

Oh knowledgeable one! Do not sleep during the day. During the night, the time between sunset and sunrise, when it is time to sleep, and even while you are asleep, do not let that time be fruitless. As for sustained attentiveness, through which one attains a proper understanding of the fact that sleep is necessary because one's body is the foundation for practicing the teaching, do not let it slip away during the time between sunset and sunrise. Continue to pay attention to positive things even during the night, which is an appropriate occasion for changing indifferent sleep into a positive quality. Sleep with the firm intention of getting up quickly in the morning to remove previously obscured ideas, so that negative things will become positive; otherwise, the time of sleep will be useless.

61 *Adopting the four immeasurable divine states of the mind which are conducive to meditation and concentration.*

Always cultivate benevolence, loving-kindness,
Joy and equanimity in the proper spirit.
Just like the One who formerly cultivated these
    indefatigably,
You will attain the pleasures of a pure world.   [*40*]

Always cultivate the four immeasurable divine states of mind in the proper spirit. The four are:
  a. Benevolence, which is to desire happiness for all beings,
  b. Loving-kindness, which is to wish that all people might be freed from their frustrations,
  c. Joy, which is to be happy when others are happy, and
  d. Equanimity, which is to encompass everything without discrimination of those near and far.
By cultivating these, ⟨23⟩ you will gain the happiness of a Brahma world, just like the past Buddhas who practiced them indefatigably.

62 *Content [of meditation and concentration].*

The four meditative levels remove
Hedonistic delight and the misery of sensuality.
One attains the same state as Brahmā,
Prabhāsvara, Śubhakṛstna, Mahāphala gods.[45]   [*41*]

The counsel that you must devote yourself to the four levels of meditation means that you ought to put into practice intense concentration which will lead you to the specific state of calm.

The first level is [threefold inasmuch as it is a counter-agent, a benefit, and a state]. *Counteragent*: First, on the level of sensuous activities, emotional instabilities, such as desiring to torment others and desiring sensuous pleasures, are removed through analysis and discursiveness.[46] *Benefit*: Then, one enjoys the joy and happiness which arise from one's solitude. *State*: A concentrated and integrated state of mind.

The second level: Through its own power, the mind eliminates analysis and discursiveness and experiences only joy and happiness.

The third level: When joy has been removed through [the attainment of] equanimity about the composite nature of things and through introspective understanding, the mind experiences only happiness.

The fourth level: Even happiness is removed through [an

---

[45] In each of the four meditative levels, one goes through various stages. In the first meditative level, one goes through the following stages:
   a. Brahmakāyika (*tshangs-ris*)
   b. Brahmapāriṣadya (*tshang-'khor*)
   c. Brahmapurohita (*tshang-pa mdun-na-'don*)
   d. Mahābrahmāṇa (*tshang-pa chen-po*)
The second meditative level consists of the following stages:
   a. Parīttābha (*'od-chung*)
   b. Apramāṇābha (*tshad-med 'od*)
   c. Ābhāsvara (*'od-gsal*)
The third meditative level consists of the following stages:
   a. Parīttaśubha (*dge-chung*)
   b. Apramāṇaśubha (*tshad-med dge*)
   c. Śubhakṛtsna (*dge-rgyas*)
The fourth level consists of the following stages:
   a. Anabhraka (*sprin-med*)
   b. Puṇyaprasava (*bsod-nams skyes; bsod-nams 'phel*)
   c. Vrihatphala (*'bras-bu che*)
See *Mvyut.* nos. CLVIII–CLXI; *see also* Lama Anagarika Govinda, *The Psychological Attitude of Early Buddhist Philosophy*, p. 176.
[46] *See* Guenther & Kawamura, *Mind in Buddhist Psychology*, p. 102.

attainment of] a pure state of equanimity and introspective understanding, and the mind attains an uncompromised state and [remains] focused on its object.

In attaining the four levels of meditation, all hedonistic delights and the miseries of sensuality are removed. By means of these four levels of meditation through which one enters the state of equanimity, which causes the removal of those things which must be removed, one becomes identical with Brahmā, Prabhāsvara, Śubhakṛtsna, and Mahāphala gods, ⟨24⟩ and succeeds in being born into this real state.[47]

63   *What one must do afterwards.*

> This consists of two parts:
>> 64. In general: The advice to accept wholesome acts and to reject negative ones.
>> 67. Specifically: The method by which one removes hindrances to mental integration.

64   *The advice to accept wholesome acts and to reject negative ones.*

> This has two parts:
>> 65. An explanation of how negative acts weigh one down while positive acts lift one up.
>> 66. The advice to produce strong positive antidotes to negative acts.

---

[47] The meaning here is that "Meditation is not only a certain practice; it is also a unique experience which does not allow itself to be projected into discursive forms . . . . Another and very important feature of Buddhist meditation is the fact that to concentrate on an object of one's choice is not the main aim or an end in itself. To become free from all ties that fetter us intellectually and emotionally is the aim, and this also includes that freedom has to be gained even from the object on which concentrated attention has been bestowed." *See* H. V. Guenther, *Philosophy and Psychology in the Abhidharma*, p. 141.

65   An explanation of how negative acts weigh one
      down while positive acts lift one up.

**Acts performed continuously, acts prompted by desires,
   acts which have no counteragent,
Acts which grow out of a precious or royal ground—
These five which are positive and negative
Are important. Strive to do the positive ones.**   [42]

Continuous performance of wholesome or unwholesome
acts; acts done with earnest desire; acts which lack aiding
forces [and as a consequence] which perpetuate themselves;
acts which grow out of a very precious ground such as [the
three] treasures; and acts which are performed on land ruled by
a king such as that from which he derives both pleasures and
pains—these five acts, which may be either positive or negative,
are more powerful than other acts. Declining to do those [ac-
tions] whose scale is small, strive to do those whose scale is
large.

66   The advice to produce strong positive antidotes to
      negative acts.

**Know that a small evil act cannot harm the
Large roots of wholesome acts, just as
An ounce of salt may change the taste of water,
But cannot change the taste of the Ganges river.**   [43]

An ounce of salt may change the taste of a small amount
of water, but it cannot change the taste of the mighty Ganges
river. In the same manner, the strength of a positive act is so
powerful that a little evil cannot harm the large and strong
roots of a wholesome act.

67   *Specifically: The method by which one removes*
      hindrances to mental integration.

Overexuberance and remorse, vindictiveness,
Gloominess and drowsiness, attachment,
      and indecision—
Know well that these five are the thieves
Who rob one of positive wealth.   [44]

Overexuberance, which is the mind getting excited over
its object, and remorse regarding acts done in the past; vindictiveness towards others; gloominess, which turns the mind in-
ward, and ⟨25⟩ drowsiness, which turns the perceptive organs
inwards; attachment, which is an interest in things which merely *seem* to be pleasing but to which one holds tenaciously; and
indecision in [committing oneself to] the path and its result—
know well that these five obscurations are thieves who rob one
of positive wealth.

Here, overexuberance and remorse are considered identical because both belong to the category of fluctuating things.
Gloominess and drowsiness are similar in that both tend to
make things dull and dim.

68   *Discernment and appreciation.*

This comprises two parts:
      69. A synopsis: The essence of the path having five
          stages of which the first is interest, and
      72. A detailed explanation: Appreciative discrimina-
          tion which is closely linked to attentiveness.

69   *The essence of the path having five stages of*
      which the first is interest.

This has two parts:
      70. An explanation of how interest and so on are to be
          adopted, and
      71. The process by which ego-inflation is overcome
          with the help of aids which are adopted.

70   *An explanation of how interest and so on are to
be adopted.*

**Confidence, assiduous striving, sustained
attentiveness,**[48] **meditative absorption, and
appreciative discrimination—
Only these five refer to the highest possible realization.
Strive after these 'unshakeable forces'
And 'controlling powers'**[49] **which become the
culminating point of the path.**   [45]

Confidence, which is the interest taken in positive things;
assiduous striving, which is to become further involved with
those positive things; sustained attentiveness, which is not to
forget the objective reference confronting one; meditative absorption, which is to focus the mind on an objective reference;
and appreciative discrimination, which is a thorough investigation of reality—these five refer to the highest possible realization, which make the path of application what it is. Strive
after these which, in the stage of patient acceptance, are called
'unshakeable forces' and which, in the stage of meditative
heat,[50] are called 'controlling powers'. They are the culminating point of the linking path[51] ⟨26⟩ because only these five can
form the link.

---

[48] *dran-pa*, 'inspection or sustained attentiveness', means "keeping the
perceptual situation as constant as possible and inspecting the objective
constituent of this situation as equitably as possible." *See* H. V. Guenther,
Treasures on the Tibetan Middle Way, p. 87, n. 1.

[49] Ibid., p. 87, n. 4: "The distinction between five controlling powers and
five (stable) forces, respectively, emphasizes the nature of meditation as a
modifiable process. The 'controlling powers' direct the course of contemplation and inform it, while the 'forces' make it continue by permeating it."

[50] The path of application (*sbyor-lam*) is divided into four parts—*drod*
(meditative heat), *rtse-mo* (maximum value), *bzod-pa* (patient acceptance)
and *'jig-rten-chos-mchog* or *lo-ka-chos-mchog* (highest worldly realization).
See rJe 'Ba'-ra-ba, *byang-chub sems-dpa'i bslab rin-po-che gter mdzod las / sa
lam drod rtags kyi yon-tan skye tshul bstan-pa*, fol. 437; and H. V. Guenther,
The Jewel Ornament of Liberation, p. 233.

[51] The translation of *sbyor-lam* by 'application' and 'linking' indicates that
this spiritual path is one of application which links one to the third path
(*mthong-lam*), the path of insight or seeing.

71   *The process by which ego-inflation is overcome*
      with the help of aids which are adopted.

One who repeatedly thinks, "I have not yet passed
      beyond
Illness, old age, birth, death, and, likewise,
Those actions by which I appropriated these features,"
Will not become ego-inflated due to counteracting
      them. [46]

One who repeatedly thinks, "I have not yet passed beyond illness, old age, birth, death, and, likewise, those actions
which have caused these frustrating situations," will not remain in the cause-and-effect pattern of frustrations because
he realizes, "I have not yet passed beyond my appropriating
these features." Therefore, he will not become ego-inflated by
assuming, "I am accomplished in mental integration and discriminative appreciation," because this way of thinking aids in
overcoming that which has to be overcome. Furthermore, it has
also been said that such a thought aids one in overcoming such
vanities as 'regarding one's status'.

72   *A detailed explanation: Appreciative*
      discrimination which is closely linked to
      attentiveness.

      This consists of two parts:
            73. An explanation that appreciative discrimination
            is the root of every proper existence, be it Saṁ-
            sāra or Nirvāṇa, and
            76. An exposition of the path of appreciative discrim-
            ination.

73   *An explanation that appreciative discrimination*
     is the root of every proper existence, be it
     Saṁsāra or Nirvāṇa.

   This has two parts:

   74. A proper understanding by worldly people which
       becomes the basis of both an elevated existence
       and liberation,[52] and
   75. An understanding by which one properly over-
       comes worldly concerns and which functions as
       the basis for liberation.[53]

74   *A proper understanding by worldly people which*
     becomes the basis of both an elevated existence
     and liberation.

   If you earnestly wish for liberation and paradise,
   You must apply yourself to acting only with a
   *   correct view.*
   If a person acts properly, but with an erroneous view,
   He will experience an excruciating outcome wherever
   *   he goes.*   [47]

   If you earnestly wish and desire to enter a state of liberation and paradise, you must apply yourself to act only with a
correct view by which you will apprehend immediately the
infallibility of cause and result in human actions. Even if a
person has, in the past, properly performed a positive act, his
erroneous view ⟨27⟩ that acts do not have their effects, will
make the positive act useless. He will experience an excruciat-

---

   [52] This concerns a proper understanding of the relation between actions
and their result (*las dang 'bras-bu*).

   [53] This refers to a proper understanding of the fact that everything *is* only
insofar as it is interrelated with everything else, and the fact that whatever *is*
is itself an 'open dimension' (*stong-pa dang rten-'brel*).

ing outcome wherever he goes and suffer the frustrations of the Hell of Uninterrupted Pain.[54]

sGrol [mgon-pa][55] states in his commentary,

> It does not seem reasonable that the outcome of an act of charity should be unpleasant and excruciating. It is so, because the little good in [a positive act] cannot be experienced when the powerful consequences of a wrong view overpower the good.

Rong [-zom][56] states in his commentary,

> The reason that anyone, who in the past has properly performed an act of giving gifts, experiences an evil and excruciating outcome is that erroneous opinions cut off wholesome acts right at their root.

75   *An understanding by which one properly overcomes worldly concerns and which functions as the basis for liberation.*

Know that men are actually unhappy,
Impermanent, without an essence, and impure.
Those who do not earnestly examine these traits,
Suffer four opinionated views which stimulate
misery.   [48]

In regard to spiritual aspirants, human beings [in particular] are actually unhappy because they are frustrated, im-

---

[54] Hell of Uninterrupted Pain: see §122ff.

[55] The name sGrol mgon-pa appears in T. V. Wylie's book, *The Geography of Tibet according to the 'Dzam-gling-rgyas-bshad*, p. 136, n. 189, as an unidentified person. Tarthang Tulku Rinpoche has supplied another possible name, sGrol-ma bsam 'grub rdo-rje.

[56] Rong is short for Rong-zom chos-kyi bzang-po, who lived in the 11th century and was one of the most influential masters in the early lineage of the Nyingma tradition. According to the *Blue Annals*, pp. 160–63, Rong-zom was the author of many books such as the *Theg-pa 'jug-pa* and, as a child, he met Atīśa. This would make him a late contemporary of Atīśa who lived from 982 to 1054 A.D.

permanent in that this moment may be their last,[57] without [independent] essence [which is considered to be] an initiator of actions, and physically impure. Those who do not look into the meaning of these traits just mentioned, suffer four opinionated views which stimulate misery: purity, happiness, permanence, and essence.

76   *An exposition of the path of appreciative discrimination.*

This consists of two parts:
77. A specific explanation of an opinionated view which inflates one, and
80. The subject matter of the path.

77   *A specific explanation of an opinionated view which inflates one.*

This has two parts:
78. An analysis of the complete personality which is devoid of a principle to which it can be reduced, and
79. An investigation of the psychophysical constituents of the personality which are the basis for assuming that a self exists as an ontological and factual reality.

78   *An analysis of the completed personality which is devoid of a principle to which it can be reduced.*

Corporeity is not the self. The self does not possess corporeity.
Corporeity does not belong to the self. Nor does the self belong to corporeity.

---

[57] bLo-bzang sbyin-pa's commentary (p. 48) reads: "impermanent because he is shattered by a single occurrence."

> *In the same manner, the other psychophysical*
>   *constituents*
> *Ought to be understood as being nothing in*
>   *themselves.*   [49]

Just as a Sūtra[58] states, "The presence of the psychophysical constituents, beginning with corporeity, etc., does not constitute a self," ⟨28⟩ so too, the self does not possess corporeity by way of an inseparable connection as exists between Devadatta and his fatness.[59] Corporeity does not belong to the self in the sense that the self is the basis of corporeity, nor does the self belong to corporeity in the sense that corporeity is the basis of a self.[60] In the same way, the other four psychophysical constituents—feelings, conceptualizations, motivating forces, and perceptual operations—ought to be understood as nothing in themselves.

79   *An investigation into the psychophysical*
>   *constituents of the personality which are at the*
>   *basis for assuming that a self exists as an*
>   *ontological and factual reality.*

> *The psychophysical constituents are not created by*
> *Sheer fancy, nor from time, nor from themselves,*
> *Nor do they pre-exist, nor come from a creator, nor are*
>   *they causeless.*
> *Know that they are produced from a loss of intrinsic*
>   *awareness and from craving.*   [50]

The psychophysical constituents, which are nothing in themselves, are not created by sheer imagination, sometimes

---

[58] This formula is found in the *Saṃyutta Nikāya*, III, 114–15.

[59] Devadatta is the name of the cousin of the Buddha. Apart from this fact, this name also figures prominently in analogies. *See* H. V. Guenther, *The Jewel Ornament of Liberation*, pp. 81, 175.

[60] 'Basis of corporeity . . . basis of a self': Tibetan text reads 'yonder basis' (*phar-rten*) and 'hither basis' (*tshur-rten*).

coming into existence on the basis of an Ātman, sometimes on the basis of something else, sometimes with a cause, and sometimes without a cause; nor are they created through the inexorable passage of time; nor are they self-realizing; nor do they pre-exist, like Brahman; nor do they come from an eternal creator god, like Iśvara; nor do they originate without a cause. Then from what? Know that they are produced when a cause (the loss of intrinsic awareness) and conditions (man's action and his craving) combine.

80   *Subject matter of the path.*

>   This consists of three parts:
>   81. Three things which are inconsistent with the path
>   and limit everything,
>   82. Assiduous striving, which is desirable, and
>   83. Training oneself to understand the essence of the
>   path.

81   *Three things which are inconsistent with the*
     path and limit everything.

>   **Attachment to ideologies based on ethical behavior and**
>   **compulsive performance,**
>   **Opinionatedness about the perishable constituents,**
>   **and indecisiveness—**
>   **Know that these three bind one completely to Saṁsāra**
>   **And close the gates to the city of liberation.**   [51]

Know that these three completely bind one to Saṁsāra and close the gates to the city of liberation:
        a. To be attached to ideologies based on objectionable
           ethical behaviors and compulsive performances,[61]

---

[61] There are five kinds of opinionatedness (*lta-ba*) of which this and the following represent two. *See* Guenther & Kawamura, *Mind in Buddhist Psychology*, pp. 74–81.

b. To be opinionated about what is perishable, which
   means to make the mistake of believing that the five
   psychophysical ⟨29⟩ constituents making up one's
   body have a primordial principle, and
c. To give way to indecision about the path and its
   effect.

82   *Assiduous striving, which is desirable.*

**As far as liberation, which depends on oneself, is
   concerned,
There is no one else who can be a friend.
Practice meditative concentration, by means of
   learning and ethical behavior,
And apply yourself to the four truths.**   [52]

As far as liberation, which depends on oneself, is concerned, if one does not rely on oneself, there is no one else, such
as a protector or guide, who can be a friend; therefore, first
intensify your awareness by listening and learning about the
Buddha's teaching, and then, while persisting in ethical behavior, practice meditative concentration through which the
mind is made lucid. Know that frustration is essential to the
path of liberation, remove its cause, become involved in actively implementing the removal [of any further causes], make
the path your very own, and apply yourself to the four noble
truths.

83   *Training oneself to understand the essence
     of the path.*

This consists of two parts:
       84. A general explanation: The three trainings, and
       85. A specific explanation: Training in appreciative
           discrimination.

84   *A general explanation: The three trainings.*[62]

**Always train yourself in supreme ethical behavior,
Supreme appreciative discrimination, and supreme
mentality.
Even the one hundred and fifty-one trainings
Are truly subsumed under these three.**   [53]

Because they are far superior to those of the heretics,
always train yourself in the three trainings of meditative concentration:
  a. Supreme ethical behavior,
  b. Supreme appreciative discrimination,
  c. Supreme mentality.[63]

What is elsewhere called 'one hundred and fifty-one trainings'
and "two hundred and fifty rules of discipline" in both ⟨30⟩ the
Mahāyāna and Hīnayāna, is truly subsumed under these three.

85   *A specific explanation: Training in appreciative
discrimination.*

This comprises two parts:
  86. The way to remove defiling factors of instability,
  151. The way to a correct realization of the purify-
     ing process.

---

[62] *bslabs-gsum*, 'the three trainings'. See Étienne Lamotte, *La Somme du
Grand Vehicule d'Asaṅga (Mahāyāna-saṃgrāha)*, tome I, pp. 68–81.

[63] 'Supreme ethical behavior' refers to ethical behaviors observed by the
seven classes of the Saṅgha (namely, *bhikṣu, bhikṣunī, śikṣamānā, śramaṇera,
śramaṇerikā, upāsaka,* and *upāsikā*). 'Supreme appreciative discrimination'
refers to the 'real' experience of the fact that both the completed individual
(*gang-zag*) and the entities of reality (*chos*) have no abiding principle to which
they can be reduced (*bdag-med*). 'Supreme mentality' refers to a holistic experience in which the mind is focused on reality (*see* bLo-bzang sbyin-pa's
commentary, p. 52).

86   *The way to remove defiling factors of instability.*

This has two parts:
87. The most appropriate action to reverse tendencies towards egocentricity in a mind involved
with this life,
103. The most appropriate action to reverse tendencies towards egocentricity in a mind involved
with the infinite extent of Saṁsāra.[64]

87   *The most appropriate action to reverse tendencies
towards egocentricity in a mind involved with
this life.*

This has two parts:
88. A summary, and
89. A detailed explanation.

88   *A summary.*

**My Lord! The Tathāgata has pointed out that
Attentiveness to the body[65] is the only path to walk.
Take hold of it, and hold on tight.
If attentiveness slips away, everything breaks
    down.   [54]**

My Lord! The Tathāgata has pointed out that attentiveness to the body is the only path to walk, because it is from there
that those who desire the path to liberation begin. It has been
stated,

---

[64] *'khor-ba mtha'-dag.* 'The infinite extent of Saṁsāra' includes the six levels
of existence.

[65] The meaning is that one must become aware of the unique occasion and
right juncture of one's existence. That these two relate to the body has been
discussed by sGam-po-pa. *See* H. V. Guenther, *The Jewel Ornament of Liberation,* p. 14; *see also* §§95–102 of this text.

Oh monks! Attentiveness to the body, the only path to walk, makes sentient beings pure, makes them pass beyond frustrations and unhappy states, makes them understand the teaching which is in accordance with reason, and makes them bring to light *Nirvāṇa*.

Therefore, acquire this attentiveness to the body and hold tightly to it, because if attentiveness slips away, everything breaks down.

89 *A detailed explanation.*

This comprises two parts:
90. Contemplation of the impermanence ⟨31⟩ of life,
95. Contemplation of the rare occurrence of the unique occasion and right juncture.[66]

90 *Contemplation of the impermanence of life.*

This has four parts:
91. Contemplation of impermanence by thinking about the uncertainty of the time of one's death.
92. Contemplation of impermanence by thinking about the fact that one is certainly going to die,
93. Contemplation of impermanence by thinking about other examples, and
94. A summary of the outcome.

91 *Contemplation of impermanence by thinking about the uncertainty of the time of one's death.*

**This life has many dangers; it is more unstable
Than a bubble blown about by the wind.**

---

[66] " 'Unique occasion' means to be free from the eight unfavourable conditions . . . . 'Right juncture' refers to five events which affect us directly and to another five occurring through others and affecting us mediately. . . . These two factors of unique occasion and right juncture meet in the precious human body." *See* H. V. Guenther, *The Jewel Ornament of Liberation*, pp. 14–16, and H. V. Guenther, *Kindly Bent to Ease Us*, pp. 3–12.

With breath coming and going, it is the greatest
Wonder that one ever awakens from sleep.   [55]

This life which has many dangers—both externally and
internally—is more unstable than a bubble blown about by the
wind; therefore, with breath coming and going, it is the greatest
wonder that one ever awakens from sleep and is still alive.

92   *Contemplation of impermanence by thinking*
     about the fact that one is certainly going to die.

The inevitable end of the body is that it turns into
     ashes,
Dries up or rots, and is a dirty heap of bones having
     nothing to it.
The limbs fall off and decompose.
Know that the body has the nature of falling
     apart.   [56]

The inevitable end of the body is that it is burned by fire
and turns to ashes, or finally dries out, or finally rots away, or
finally becomes a dirty heap of bones having nothing to it. The
body rots away when the major and minor limbs fall off and
decompose by dissipating into atoms. From now on, know that
the body has the nature of falling apart.

93   *Contemplation of impermanence by thinking*
     about other examples.

If even the earth, Mt. Sumeru, and the ocean are
Destroyed by the burning fires of the seven suns,[67]
And these to the point that not even a piece of ash
     remains,
Then why think that man, who is so frail,
     is permanent?   [57]

---

[67] Reference to this event can be found in *Abhidharmakośa*, III, 90. *See*
Louis de la Vallée Poussin, *L'Abhidharmakośa de Vasubandhu*, III, p. 184;
Lin Li-Kouang, *op. cit.*, VII, 26, p. 115; *Aṅguttara*, VII, 62; *Buddhacarita*,
XX, 26.

If even the earth, Mt. Sumeru, and the great ocean, which appear so solid and firm, are destroyed by the fires of the seven suns ⟨32⟩ at the end of a *kalpa*,[68] and even though these have solid foundations and forms yet are destroyed to the point that not even a piece of ash remains, then why think that man, who is so frail and bound to be destroyed, is permanent?

94   A *summary of the outcome.*

> *Everything is impermanent and without an abiding*
> *   principle;*
> *Since there is no assistant, no protector, and no*
> *   foundation,*
> *You, honorable sir, should let yourself become*
> *   disgusted*
> *With Saṁsāra, which is like a banana tree.*   [58]

Everything, whether external or internal, is impermanent and without an abiding principle; and thus, since there is no assistant who can help you out of frustrations, no protector who can be of benefit to you, nor any shrine in which you can make your refuge, let your mind, honorable sir, become disgusted with Saṁsāra, which, like the banana tree, is without a core, and free yourself from Saṁsāra.

95   *Contemplation of the rare occurrence of the*
      unique occasion and right juncture.

This consists of three parts:
>   96. General explanation: Preciousness of having become a human being,
>   99. Specific explanation: Sites in which four opportune interactions take place which provide favorable conditions, and
>   102. Think about how to remove the eight obstacles to happiness, which create unfavorable conditions.

---

[68] According to the *Abhidharmakośa*, p. 182, this *kalpa* is called *saṁvartakalpa*.

96   *Preciousness of having become a human being.*

This has two parts:
      97. Why birth as a human being is precious, and
      98. Why performing an evil act in one's existence is
          something very bad.

97   *Why birth as a human being is precious.*

Since to attain human existence after existence
    as an animal
Is more difficult than for a turtle to put its neck
Into a hole of a yoke tossed about in an ocean,
Make life fruitful, oh King, by acting properly.   [59]

To attain human existence, after having been liberated
from existence as an animal, is more difficult than for a turtle to
put its neck into a hole of a yoke tossed about by the waves of a
great ocean. Therefore, make your life fruitful, ⟨33⟩ Oh King,
by acting properly.

98   *Why performing an evil act in one's existence is*
    something very bad.

He who does evil acts after having become a human
Is more foolish than one who collects
A stinking pile of vomit
In a precious gold vessel.   [60]

He who does unwholesome evil acts after having become
a human being is more stupid than one who, because he collects
a stinking pile of vomit in a gold vessel studded with precious
jewels, is called 'foolish'.[69]

---

[69] The image here is that man does not realize the significance of human
life.

99   *Specific explanation:*

This consists of two parts:
   100. In general, an explanation of the four opportune
         interactions,
   101. In particular, an explanation of spiritual friends.

100   *In general, an explanation of the four opportune
      interactions.*

> **To dwell in a favorable place, to associate**
> **With worthy people, to practice true devotion, and**
> **To possess good merits of previous lives—**
> **These four great opportune interactions enable you**
> **   to attain your purpose in life.**   **[61]**

Living in a place favorable to the emergence of the noble
path, that is, to dwell among men and gods; association with
worthy people; devotion in which you yourself truly wish to
travel the path to liberation; good merits acquired in previous
lives which brought you to the path—since these impelling
forces are the great wheels which draw the wagon of the noble
path, they are the four great opportune interactions. They
enable you to attain your purpose in life. You [Oh King! are
fortunate to] possess them already.

101   *In particular, an explanation of spiritual friends.*

> **The Buddha has said, "The pure act[70] of relying**
> **On a spiritual friend is perfect!"**
> **Rely on a spiritual friend, because by relying on**
> **   an accomplished Buddha,**
> **Many have attained calm.**   **[62]**

---

[70] *tshangs-par-spyod-pa (brahmacārya)*, the 'pure act'. In the Yoga system
in India, *brahmacārya* means to refrain from sexual acts. The teachings of the
Buddha, however, emphasize reliance on Dharma friends since they provide
the necessary conditions for complete enlightenment. For the relation of this
passage to the teaching of the Prajñāpāramitā, *see* bLo-bzang sbyin-pa's
commentary, pp. 61–62.

Furthermore, reliance on a spiritual friend is a pure act. 'Pure' means beyond emotional needs and 'act' means the path. Thus the Buddha said, "Only that [pure act] is perfect!" Because Ānanda asked, "Oh Bhagavat, ⟨34⟩ are Dharma teachers and Dharma friends norms for the pure act?" the Buddha replied, "Don't put it that way! They bring to perfection the pure act."

Therefore, rely on a spiritual friend, because by relying on an accomplished Buddha, many sentient beings have attained calm.

102   *Think about how to remove the eight obstacles to*
      happiness, which create unfavorable conditions.

      To entertain an erroneous view, to be born among
      The animals, spirits, and denizens of hell,
      To be born a savage in a far-off place where there is no
         Dharma,
      To be born a dumb person or a long-living god—   [63]

      Any one of these births is unsatisfactory.
      These therefore comprise the eight obstacles.
      After having encountered a satisfactory juncture
         free of them,
      Endeavor to avert the possibility of (re)birth.   [64]

To entertain an erroneous view, which denies the relationship between a cause and its effect; to be born among the animals; or among the spirits; or among the denizens of hell; to be born among the savages in a far-off place where there is no Dharma; or to be born in a period when there is no Buddha, so that one cannot hear the teaching; even if a Buddha should appear, to be born a dumb person or a mute with physical or mental defects; or to be born a long-living god who has no faculty for thinking—birth in any one of these eight situations is an obstacle to happiness. Therefore, there are eight obstacles.

After becoming freed from them and thus encountering a satisfactory unique juncture, from then on, endeavor to avert the possibility of (re)birth into Saṁsāra, and you will not be born there again.

103 *The most appropriate action to reverse tendencies*
     towards egocentricity in a mind involved with
     the infinite extent of Saṁsāra.

The most appropriate action is to make the mind reflect ⟨35⟩ on the evils of Saṁsāra. This comprises two parts:
     104. Synopsis, and
     105. A detailed explanation.

104 A *synopsis.*

My Lord, get disgusted with Saṁsāra wherein you
Become depressed through desires and wherein many
Frustrations such as sickness and old age arise.
Even if you know how bad things are, you must still
     listen.   [65]

Why must (re)birth be averted? My Lord, since Saṁsāra is a state in which you become depressed through desiring such things as clothes and food, and end up with death, while in the meantime many frustrations such as sickness and old age arise —you should become disgusted with it! When Saṁsāra is talked about—even if you know how miserable it is—listen carefully!

105 A *detailed explanation.*

This consists of two parts:
     106. Although everything seems as it should be, one
          cannot be certain, and
     119. The wide and awesome extent of frustrations.

106   *Although everything seems as it should be, one*
       cannot be certain.

This has two parts:
   107. The ways in which the mind is unstable, and
   118. The advice to gain a positive attitude from know-
        ing about this instability.

107   *The ways in which the mind is unstable.*

This has four parts:
   108. Because there is no certainty about who are en-
        emies and who are friends, the mind is unstable,
   109. Because there is nothing which can satisfy, the
        mind is unstable,
   110. Because of the uncertainty of the hereafter, the
        mind is unstable, and
   111. Because of the uncertainty of a high or low [sta-
        tus], the mind is unstable.

108   *Because there is no certainty about who are*
       enemies and who are friends, the mind is
       unstable.

   A father is a son, a mother is a wife,
   A man becomes an enemy and then a friend,
   Or vice-versa; therefore, there is
   No certainty whatsoever in Saṁsāra.   **[66]**

   A father is a son, a mother is a wife, a man becomes an
enemy and then a friend, and conversely, a friend becomes an
enemy; therefore, ⟨36⟩ there is no certainty whatsoever in
Saṁsāra.

109   *Because there is nothing which can satisfy, the
      mind is unstable.*

      **Know that each person has drunk more milk
      Than that contained in the four oceans.
      But know that he will drink still more,
      While he follows the ordinary paths.**   [67]

Each person has drunk plenty of milk, more than that
contained in the four great oceans,[71] and yet he is not satisfied
and has not attained the noble path. But know that in Saṁsāra,
he will drink much more than that while he follows the ordi-
nary paths, because there is no beginning or end to Saṁsāra.

110   *Because of the uncertainty of the hereafter, the
      mind is unstable.*

      **The heap of bones of a single human being far
        surpasses Mt. Sumeru in height.
      If each mother, in the lineage of mothers,
      Were considered as a pill the size of a juniper seed,
      The earth could not contain their number.**   [68]

The heap of bones discarded from the previous births of a
single human being, far surpasses Mt. Sumeru in height, yet if
one does not exert himself on the path, he will need even more
births. In the same way, if each mother, in the lineage of
mothers, were considered as a pill, as small as the seed of the
juniper plant, the earth could not contain their number. The
Buddha, referring only to the bodies of those born from a
womb,[72] states,

----
[71] The 'four great oceans' refer to the four oceans surrounding Mt. Sumeru.
[72] Three other kinds of birth are: oviparous, moisture generated, and spontaneous birth.

Oh Bhikṣus! Suppose a person takes a pill the size of a juniper seed from this great earth and, saying, "This is my mother, this is my mother's mother," takes a count of them. Then, Oh Bhikṣus, this great mound of earth will become quickly exhausted, but the lineage of people's mothers is never exhausted.

Mothers have been the sustaining force of human embodiment, over and over again. ⟨37⟩

111   *Because of the uncertainty of a high or low*
[status] the mind is unstable.

This consists of six parts:
112. One cannot trust anything in the whole universe,
113. One cannot trust pleasant companions,
114. One cannot trust pleasant situations,
115. One cannot trust pleasant surroundings,
116. One cannot trust anything pleasurable, and
117. One cannot trust an established status or sphere.

112   *One cannot trust anything in the whole universe.*

Even after having become the praiseworthy Indra,
By the power of one's Karma, one falls to earth again.
Even after having become an universal monarch,
One becomes a servant in the flow of Saṁsāra.   [69]

Even after having become the praiseworthy Indra, the king of gods, by the power of one's Karma, one falls to earth again. Even after having become an universal monarch, the ruler of men, if no previous wholesome qualities remain, one becomes a servant once more, like a slave to slaves, in the flow of Saṁsāra.

113 *One cannot trust pleasant companions.*

> **Even after having enjoyed, for a long time, the
> pleasures of
> Fondling the breasts and waists of the daughters of
> heaven,
> One has to experience, in hell, the unendurable pains of
> Being smashed and cut up by jagged-edged rotating
> wheels.** [70]

Even after having enjoyed, for a long time, the pleasures of fondling the breasts and waists of the goddesses of the heavenly world, one has to experience, in hell, the unendurable pains of being smashed between two mountains and cut up by swords and jagged-edged rotating wheels, which are like the fangs and claws of iron dogs.

114 *One cannot trust pleasant situations.*

> **Even after having remained a long time on the
> summit of Mt. Sumeru,
> Where one enjoyed one's strolls,
> Again, one experiences the intolerable pains of
> walking in
> The Hell of Fire Pit and the Hell of Dirty
> Swamp.** [71]

Even after having remained a long time, as long as one thousand god-years[73] on the summit of Mt. Sumeru, where one enjoyed walking on precious ground which yields underfoot, again, by the power of one's Karma, one experiences the intolerable pains and frustrations of walking ⟨38⟩ in the Hell of Fire Pit and the Hell of Dirty Swamp, in which one sinks up to his knees.

---

[73] *lha'i-lo*, 'god-year'. The sense of time is a function of one's environment.

115   *One cannot trust pleasant surroundings.*

> *Having enjoyed the pleasures of chasing the daughters*
> *Of heaven and of a life in a beautiful garden, again,*
> *One gets one's legs, hands, ears, and nose slashed off*
> *By branches of garden trees similar to sticks and*
> *swords.*   [72]

> *Having sat together with the goddesses of heaven*
> *On a cushion of golden lotus petals, in a*
> *Gently flowing stream, again, one falls into the*
> *Intolerably hot salt river, the Vaitaraṇī, in hell.*   [73]

The Indian commentary (*rGya-'grel*)[74] states, " 'To chase'
means 'to hold close to one'." Therefore, having enjoyed the
pleasures of chasing and holding close the beautiful goddesses
of heaven, one again gets legs, hands, ears, and nose slashed off
by the branches of garden trees which are similar to sticks and
swords.

Having sat together with the beautiful goddesses of heav-
en on a cushion of golden lotus petals, one again falls into the
Vaitaraṇī, an intolerably hot river of putrid, impure brine, in
the terrible existence of hell.

116   *One cannot trust great pleasures.*

> *Even after having obtained the great pleasures of*
> *heaven*
> *And the bliss of Brahmahood, free of desires,*
> *One has once again to suffer unending*
> *Pains by becoming fuel in Avīci Hell.*[75]   [74]

Even after having obtained the great pleasures of heaven
and the bliss of Brahmahood, free of desires, one has once again
to suffer unending and uninterrupted pain by becoming fuel in
Avīci Hell.

---

[74] The 'Indian commentary' refers to Mahāmati's *Vyaktapadāsuhṛllekhaṭīkā*
(P. ed., vol. 129, no. 5690).
[75] Avīci is the worst of all hells; *see* §130.

117   *One cannot trust an established status or sphere.*

> **Having attained the state of the sun and moon, one**
> **illumines**
> **The corners of the world with the light of one's**
> **own body.**
> **Yet still, one reaches the obscurities of darkness and**
> **Cannot see one's own hands even if one stretches**
> **them out.   [75]**

Having attained the state of the sun and moon—the sons
of gods—one illumines the corners of the world with ⟨39⟩ the
light of one's own body, the abode of the gods. Yet still, one
reaches the obscurities of darkness between the mythical conti-
nents and cannot see one's own hands, even if one holds them
out before one's eyes.

Therefore, even those who acquired a good existence
became the same as those who were born into a painful existence, because they did not have the capacity to remain there.
It was not due to the fact that a change from one situation to
another had to be a painful one. Those who do not attain the
sublime path roam about in evil existences as a consequence of
their own acts. This means that a later situation results when
the impelling forces of a prior act become exhausted.

118   *The advice to gain a positive attitude from*
      knowing about this instability.

> **Knowing that such activities produce frustrations,**
> **Take hold of happiness which is the light produced**
> **by the three lamps.**
> **Know that one enters alone the infinite darkness**
> **Which even the sun and moon cannot illumine.   [76]**

Knowing that such activities produce frustrations in this
world, take hold of happiness which is the light produced by

the three lamps—that is, charity, ethical behavior, and contemplation—which dispel the darkness of an evil existence. Why? Because if one becomes separated from the light of happiness, one enters, all alone, the infinite darkness of Saṁsāra which even the sun and moon cannot illumine, and there one experiences ⟨40⟩ excruciating and intolerable pains.

119   *The wide and awesome extent of frustrations.*

>This consists of two parts:
>120. One must know that Saṁsāra simply means being frustrated, and
>148. The advice that one must make efforts to avert the possibility of (re)birth, by knowing Saṁsāra.

120   *One must know that Saṁsāra simply means being frustrated.*

>This has five parts:[76]
>121. Frustrations in hell,
>134. Frustrations in the realm of animals,
>137. Frustrations in the realm of spirits,
>144. Frustrations in the realm of gods, and
>147. Frustrations in the realm of demigods.

---

[76] It is of interest to note here that Mi-pham lists only five levels of beings in his discussion of Saṁsāra. The reason for this is that these five levels of beings are projections of one's mind. Outside of the way in which man views his world, there is no place like hell, the realm of animals, spirits, gods, and demigods. This may seem contradictory to what one observes in the world because one actually sees cows and horses, for example, wandering about and grazing in the fields. Were the teachings of the Buddha meant to establish the existence or non-existence of such 'external' objects, then it would have failed drastically; but obviously, this is not the purpose of the teaching. Here, in dealing with the five realms, pointers or indicators are given to show the various emotional states which make up the dynamic process of man's mind. Caution must be exercised in reading these sections devoted to the various frustrations of Saṁsāra so that one will not perpetuate the idea that Buddhism establishes and deals with realms outside the logical fictions of one's mind.

121   *Frustrations in hell.*

>   This has two parts:
>   122. A presentation, and
>   123. An explanation.

122   *A presentation.*

>   **Beings who perform evil actions will always experience**
>   **Frustrations in hells such as the Hell of Reviving, the**
>   **Hell of Black Thread, the Hell of Intense Heat, Hell of**
>   **Crushing, Hell of Howling, and Hell of Uninterrupted**
>   **Pain.[77]   [77]**

Beings who perform evil acts in the three gateways[78] will suffer in both hot and cold hells such as the Hell of Reviving, the Hell of Black Thread, the Hell of Intense Heat, the Hell of Crushing, the Hell of Howling, and the Hell of Uninterrupted Pain.

123   *An explanation.*

>   This consists of two parts:
>   124. The advice to get to know frustrations, and
>   133. The advice to remove their cause.

124   *The advice to get to know frustrations.*

>   This has two parts:
>   125. Frustrations, and
>   126. Reflection on how and where they come about.

---

[77] For an explanation of these hells *see* Mi-pham's *mKhas-'jug*, fol. 35a, and dPal-sprul's *Khrid-yig*, fols. 43a–48a.

[78] 'Three gateways': *see* n. 10.

125   *Frustrations.*

> **Some are pressed like sesame seed, and**
> **Others are crushed to dust like fine flour.**   [78a,b]

Some beings, born into the Hell of Crushing, are pressed like sesame seeds between two iron plates. In the same way, others are put into a burning iron mortar and crushed to a fine flour-like dust with iron pestles.

> **Some are carved into pieces with saws, and**
> **Others are cut up with excruciatingly sharp**
> **axes.**   [78c,d]

In the Hell of Black Thread, some are carved into pieces with saws, and others are cut up with excruciatingly sharp axes. ⟨41⟩

> **Flaming liquid waves of molten bronze**
> **Are poured into others.**   [79a,b]

Likewise, others, on the bank of the river Vaitaraṇī, are made to drink flaming liquid waves of molten bronze, which are poured into their mouths.

> **Some are completely fastened**
> **With burning iron pins to a spiked wall.**   [79c,d]

Some in the Hell of Heat are completely fastened, like flowers, with burning iron pins to a spiked wall.

> **Some are thrown to the ground by dogs**
> **with iron fangs**
> **And lie with outstretched arms.**   [80a,b]

Some, in the forest of pointed swords, having been thrown on the ground and frightened by dogs with iron fangs, lie terrified with outstretched arms.

Others suffer helplessly, being clawed by crows
With sharp iron beaks and intolerable claws.   [80c,d]

There too, others made powerless because of their own Karma, are picked at and clawed by birds with sharp iron beaks and crows with intolerable claws.

Some wail and roll about, while various worms and
    beetles,
And myriad bluebottles and bees with long stings
Open up wounds painful even to the touch,
And begin to feast on them.   [81]

In the Neighboring Hells, some wail and roll their painful bodies about, while worms, which crawl out of the body, and beetles of various different colors, shapes, and kinds coming from the outside, and myriad bluebottles and black bees [with long stings] open up wounds, painful even to the touch, and begin to feast on them.

Some stand open-mouthed in a heap
Of live coals which burn uninterruptedly.   [82a,b]

Some, in the Hell of Heat, are open-mouthed, as they stand in a heap of live coals which burn uninterruptedly—and they are powerless to leave.

Some are cast head down into iron kettles,
Like the ingredients of rice soup, and are
    cooked.   [82c,d]

In the Hell of Intense Heat, ⟨42⟩ others are cast head down into a burning iron kettle, like the ingredients of rice soup, and are cooked—thus they suffer greatly.

126   *Reflection on how and where they come about.*

This consists of three parts:
  127. Reflection on the time during which pain comes
  about,
  128. Reflection on how intolerable it is, when it takes
  place, and
  132. Reflection on the length of time one experiences
  pain.

127   *Reflection on the time during which pain comes
about.*

**Adamantine, indeed, is the heart of an evil doer, who
Has heard of the thousand ways in which those whose
Breathing has stopped suffer immeasurable pains
In hell and yet is not frightened by them.**   [83]

Solid like a diamond is the heart of any evil doer, who has
heard of the thousand ways in which those who die when their
breathing has stopped or has been cut off suffer immeasurable
and intolerable pains in hell, and who is yet neither frightened
by them nor dreads them.

128   *Reflection on how intolerable pain is when it
takes place.*

This consists of three parts:
  129. In general,
  130. In specific, and
  131. An analogy.

129   *In general.*

**If fear is produced even by seeing a picture, or
By hearing, by thinking, by reciting, or
By making statues of hellish beings, what is there to
Say about the actual experience of an intolerable
    situation?**   [84]

If, from descriptions of or by seeing painted pictures of hell, or by hearing stories about hell with one's own ears, or by thinking about it in one's own mind, or by reciting from one's own memory, or by making statues of hellish beings out of clay, one is frightened, what is there to say about one's actual experience of an intolerable situation?

130   *In specific.* ⟨43⟩

> *Just as, of all positive qualities, the*
> *Extinction of a potential life-form is called 'the Lord',*
> *So too, in the same manner, of all painful things,*
> *Avīci Hell is called 'the most intolerable'.*   [85]

Of all pleasant things, the outcome of liberation, which is a complete extinction of the three levels of a potential life-form, is called 'a wholesome power' or 'the Lord'; so too, in the same manner, of all painful things, Avīci Hell is called 'the most intolerable'.

131   *An analogy.*

> *Frustrations produced when fearful enemies in this*
> *World shoot three hundred arrows in a single day*
> *Neither equal a fraction of nor illustrate*
> *The smallest pain in hell.*   [86]

Frustrations produced in the world of man when, in a single day, three hundred arrows are continuously shot by fearful and powerful enemies would not equal nor illustrate the smallest part of what one will have to suffer in hell.

132   *Reflection on the length of time one experiences pain.*

> *Those very intolerable pains are*
> *Experienced for one hundred times ten million years,*

But as long as pain is not extinguished,
One will not be freed from that existence.   [87]

Those very intolerable pains explained previously, are experienced for one hundred times ten million years, but as long as the causes which produce pain are not extinguished, one will not be freed from that existence and will experience pain throughout that time.

133   *The advice to remove its cause.*

You must skillfully apply yourself to avoid
Even the most minute evil act, because
The seeds of those unhappy states are evil acts
Done by body, speech, and mind.   [88]

To remove the cause of pain, Oh Great King, you must skillfully apply yourself to avoid even the most minute evil act, because the seeds of those unhappy states, which are discussed above, are the grave and evil acts performed by the body, such as killing, by speech, such as lying, and by the mind, such as greedy desire. ⟨44⟩

134   *Frustrations in the realm of animals.*

This consists of two parts:
    135. Frustrations in general, and
    136. Distinct and separate frustrations.

135   *Frustrations in general.*

If one is born an animal, there are various pains
Such as being killed, tied up, and struck.
Those who cast aside the positive qualities of calm
Suffer unbearable pains that result from eating one
    another.   [89]

If one is born on the level of an animal, there are various pains which men and gods inflict to cause hurt, such as killing, tying with a rope, and striking with chains. Those who cast aside the positive qualities of the path to liberation by which one attains the calm of Nirvāṇa, suffer unbearable pain, like that caused by fish eating one another.

136 *Distinct and separate frustrations.*

> *Some animals are killed for pearls,*
> *Wool, bones, meat, and hide.*
> *Helpless, others are kicked, coralled,*
> *Chained, whipped, and thus are they used.* [90]

Some, living in watery places, are killed for pearls; sheep are killed for wool, elephants for ivory and blood, wild animals for meat, tigers and leopards for their hides. Helpless others, like horses, are kicked; cattle and buffalo are corralled; donkeys are whipped; elephants are chained and struck with blows of the stick; used in this manner as slaves, they suffer.

137 *Frustrations in the realm of spirits.* ⟨45⟩

This consists of two parts:
  138. A presentation, and
  139. An explanation.

138 *A presentation.*

> *Because frustrations produced from insatiable*
>   *desires are never ending,*
> *Birth into the realm of the spirits is the starting point*
> *For unendurable frustrations produced by*
> *Hunger, thirst, cold, heat, having to wander, and*
>   *fear.* [91]

Because the frustrations produced by insatiable desires are continuous, never ending, and a natural part of a life as a spirit, birth into the realm of the spirits is the starting point for unendurable frustrations produced by hunger, thirst, cold winters, hot summers, having to wander about for food, and the fears occasioned when one sees men take up arms.

139   *An explanation.*

This consists of two parts:
140. Pain, and
143. Cause of pain.

140   *Pain.*

This consists of two parts:
141. Actual pain, and
142. Length of time one experiences pain.

141   *Actual pain.*

Because some have mouths the size of a needle's eye
And stomachs the size of mountains, they are
        tormented,
But they do not have the energy to eat
Even a morsel of food thrown on miserable filth.   [92]

Because some spirits have mouths the size of a needle's eye, but their stomachs, being as large as mountains, are difficult to fill, they are tormented by insatiable hunger. But they do not have the energy to eat even a useless morsel of food [which has been] thrown away [as if it were] miserable filth such as pus.

Some, whose bodies are of skin and bones,
        stand naked, and
Look like the dried top of a Tāla tree.   [93a,b]

Some, whose skin and bones are all that, externally and internally, is left of their body, and whose flesh is dried out, stand naked and without clothing and look like the weathered top of a Tāla tree.

Others have fire shooting out of their mouth
  throughout the night,
And eat sand which falls into their burning
  mouth as food.   [93c,d]

Others have fire shooting out of their mouth throughout the whole night and, even if they eat food, ⟨46⟩ they find themselves eating sand which falls into their burning mouth.

Some, an unfortunate lot, do not get even
Filth such as pus, excrement, or blood.
They pierce each others' faces until their necks
Swell, and then eat the ripened pus.   [94]

Some, who live in an unfortunate state, do not get even stinky pus or excrement or rotten blood, and, out of anger, they beat each other with hammers and pierce each others' faces until their necks swell, and then eat the ripened pus. In this way, they continue to live.

To the spirits, even the moon seems hot in the summer
And the sun feels cold in the winter.
A tree in paradise becomes fruitless,
And if they should even so much as look at rivers,
  these dry up.   [95]

For the spirits, misery arises because even the moon seems hot in the summer, while the sun feels cold in the winter. Even a beautiful tree in paradise becomes fruitless when they look at it, and if they should even so much as look at rivers, these dry up.

142   *The length of time one experiences pain.*

> **Since the potential for evil acts**
> **Which is the basis for uninterrupted misery**
> **Is strong, a person who is bound up in this state**
> **Will not overcome it even in five thousand**
> **years.**   [96]

Since the potential for evil acts which is the basis for uninterrupted misery is very strong, a person who is bound up in this state will not overcome it even in five thousand years, and he will experience frustrations.

143   *Cause of pain.*

> **The Buddha has declared that a person who rejoices**
> **in avarice,**
> **Which is not a quality of noble people,**
> **Is the cause of any experience which is similar to**
> **The various miseries suffered by those in the realm of**
> **the spirits.**   [97]

The Buddha has declared that a person who rejoices in avarice is the cause of any situation which is experienced as, or is similar in nature to, the various miseries such as hunger and thirst suffered by spirits. Avarice is a quality of those who think ⟨47⟩ 'I have nothing' and is not practiced by noble people. The *sDud-pa* (*Saṁcayagāthapañjika*) states,

> One who has avarice will be born into the realm of the spirits. Even if one should be born a man, his life will be poverty-stricken.

144   *Frustrations in the realm of gods.*

> This consists of two parts:
>   145. A presentation, and
>   146. An explanation.

145   *A presentation.*

> *The pleasures of heaven may be great,*
> *But the pain of their extinction will be even greater.*
> *Therefore, supreme beings understand this and*
> *Do not desire a heaven which comes to an end.*   [98]

When one attains birth as a Kāmadeva in heaven, one may derive great pleasures from conduct that yields the highest quality of satisfaction, but on account of their intensity, the pain of death will be even greater in intensity than the previous pleasures. Therefore, reflecting on this fact, supreme beings do not desire a heaven which comes to an end, because this pleasure is not stable.

146   *An explanation.*

> *The color of the body turns ugly, one's cushion becomes*
> *Unbearable, the wreath of flowers decays, clothing*
> *Becomes soiled, and perspiration which was not*
> *There previously appears on the body.*   [99]

> *These five signs, which signify death in heaven,*
> *Appear to the gods residing in heaven and*
> *Are the same signs which signify*
> *Death to men who live on earth.*   [100]

When the gods die, the color of their bodies becomes ugly; their cushions, however comfortable they may have been previously, at this time become unbearable; the ornamental wreath of flowers decays; clothing becomes soiled; and perspiration, which was previously absent, appears on the body. These five signs, which indicate death to the gods in heaven, appear to the gods residing in heaven ⟨48⟩ and are the same signs which signify death to men who live on earth.

If there is nothing good in those
Who die in the world of gods,
They inevitably attain one or other of these existences
As animals, spirits, or hellish beings.   [101]

But that's not all! If there is no good in those who die in the world of gods, which can cause them to be (re)born into heaven, then they inevitably attain one or other of these existences as animals, spirits, or hellish beings, and come to experience misery.

147   *Frustrations in the realm of demigods.*

Even demigods, by nature, perceive the happiness
of gods,
And therefore, are very unhappy.
Even if they have intelligence,
They cannot see the truth due to the
obscurations of their level of being.   [102]

The happiness of the gods is apparent to those who are born into the realm of the demigods due to their Karma, which is caused by jealousy. Since jealousy produces unhappiness, the demigods are very unhappy. Even if they have intelligence, they cannot see the truth of their own existence due to the obscurations of their situation and their level of being.

148   *The advice that one must make efforts to avert*
        the possibility of (re)birth, by knowing Saṁsāra.

This consists of two parts:
        149. The reason one must change one's life, and
        150. The advice that one must quickly change one's
              life, because of that reason.

149 *The reason one must change one's life.*

Since Saṁsāra is such that either among gods or men,
Or among hellish beings, spirits, or animals,
There is no happy birth, know that birth
In these existences embodies much harm. [103]

Since the natural state of Saṁsāra includes all those defects which have already been described, birth as gods, men, hellish beings, spirits, or animals is not a pleasant thing. Therefore, know that birth ⟨49⟩ into any one of those existences embodies much harm, like terror and frustration.

150 *The advice that one must quickly change one's*
     life because of that reason.

If one's hair or clothing suddenly caught on fire,
One would throw everything away to extinguish it.
Similarly, one must strive to avoid worldly concerns,
Because there is nothing more important. [104]

Therefore, just as when one's hair or clothing has suddenly caught on fire, one has to extinguish it quickly, a sage who knows the evil state of Saṁsāra, in order to put out the fire [of Saṁsāra], throws away even the practice of assiduous striving; therefore, he does away with worldly concerns by cultivating assiduity which is not concerned with a body or a life. Therefore, make up your mind to avert the possibility of (re)birth in the same way as the sages, because there is nothing more important and pressing than to do away with worldly concerns.

151   *The way to a correct realization of the purifying*
       process.

This has two parts:
    152. One must be confident of liberation,[79] which is
        the goal, and
    153. One must experience the truth of the path, which
        is the cause.

152   *One must be confident of liberation, which is the*
       goal.

You must, by ethical behavior, appreciative
discrimination, and mental integration,
Strive to attain the controlled and pure citadel of
Nirvāṇa
Which has nothing to do with old age or death
[and] which
Is freed from earth, fire, wind, sun, and moon.   [*105*]

The three precious trainings, namely, ethical behavior,
appreciative discrimination, and mental integration, cause frustrations to grow calm, and this is what is meant by the word
'Nirvāṇa', which is the goal, the ageless and deathless citadel.
This citadel, which is pure because the emotions have been
removed, and which is a controlled [state] because Karma
which binds one to a possible existence has been exhausted, is
ageless and deathless, because it has nothing to do with old age
and death. You must attain that which is beyond ⟨50⟩ things
like earth, water, fire, wind, sun, and moon, which constitute
the static liberation postulated by non-Buddhists.

---

[79] It must be kept in mind that liberation, for the Buddhists, is no static end.
The way, or the going, is itself the goal, and hence, the goal is a refining
process.

Here, 'Nirvāṇa which is the highest state of calm' is one in which the psychophysical constituents, which are bound to break, are no more. 'Nirvāṇa in which something is still left to be subdued' is one in which the senses still have to be subdued. Both kinds of Nirvāṇa are pure, because they are freed from emotions.

153   *One must experience the truth of the path, which*
      is the cause.

This consists of two parts:
   154. The path of seeing, and
   163. The path of developing the vision.

154   *The path of seeing.*

This has two parts:
   155. An explanation that the way as such consists of the seven constituent members of enlightenment, and
   156. Specifically, an explanation of the profound meditative practice of appreciative discrimination which is intimately related to calmness.

155   *An explanation that the way as such consists of*
      the seven constituent members of enlightenment.

Attentiveness, a thorough investigation of reality,
   energy,
Joy, alertness, meditative absorption, and
   equanimity are
The seven constituent members of enlightenment,
   and are
Healthy accumulations whereby one attains
   Nirvāṇa.   **[106]**

When one is on the path of seeing—attentiveness, which does not let an objective reference slip away from the mind; appreciative discrimination, which thoroughly investigates reality; energy, which is the endeavor to do what is acceptable and to avoid what must be rejected; joy, which is a happy state of the mind; alertness, which gives fluency to bodily and mental acts; meditative absorption, which is a holistic experience in which the mind is kept focused on its objective reference; equanimity, which is freedom from depression and elation— these are called the 'seven constituent members of enlightenment'. Here, 'enlightenment' means Nirvāṇa, and 'constituent members' refers to what is in agreement with Nirvāṇa. Therefore, these constituent members of enlightenment become the most appropriate actions for realizing Nirvāṇa. Moreover,

a. Appreciative discrimination, which directly apprehends the fact that there is no principle to which a thing can be reduced, is the constituent member which denotes the actuality of enlightenment, because it is the very essence of enlightenment.

b. ⟨51⟩ Attentiveness is the constituent member which denotes its presence.

c. Energy is the constitutent member which determines the certainty that one will become freed from Saṁsāra.

d. Joy is the constituent member denoting the benefit derived.

e. The other three are constituent members which remove emotions.

Therefore, these seven are the healthy accumulations which make one realize Nirvāṇa.

156   *Specifically, an explanation of the profound meditative practice of appreciative discrimination which is intimately related to calmness.*

This consists of two parts:

157. A dictum, and
158. An explanation.

157   A *dictum.*

*In the absence of appreciative discrimination, there is
no concentration.
In the absence of concentration, there is no
appreciative discrimination.
Know that to one who possesses both, the ocean of a
Potential life-form is like a hoof-print.*   [107]

In the absence of appreciative discrimination, which is
discriminative of the entities of reality, there is no concentration which becomes the factor which causes supreme liberation. Through concentration one remains in a state of
equanimity about a thing which appreciative discrimination
has apprehended directly. In the absence of concentration,
there is no appreciative discrimination, which makes a real
experience out of the path to liberation, because knowledge
about reality comes after the mind has entered the state of
equanimity.

Therefore, know that to a person who has both appreciative discrimination and concentration, which are in unity
with the state of calm and with a wide perspective,[80] even the
great ocean of a potential life-form, across which one cannot
see, is like the scant water found in a dried and hardened
hoof-print. Since a person, who is calm and has a wide perspective [is free from expectations and fears], it is not difficult
for him to dry up the ocean of Saṁsāra.

158   *An explanation.*

This consists of two parts:
159. An explanation of hazy views ⟨52⟩ which render
       nonsensical that which must be cultivated, and
160. An explanation of dependent origination, which
       properly counteracts hazy views.

---

[80] Calm is the essence of concentration, while a wide perspective is the
essence of appreciative discrimination. *See* H. V. Guenther, *Jewel Ornament
of Liberation*, p. 197, and H. V. Guenther, *Kindly Bent to Ease Us*, p. 191.

159   *An explanation of hazy views*[81] *which render*
       nonsensical that which must be cultivated.

Śākyamuni Buddha has stated that none of the
Fourteen hazy views about the world
Should be considered, because
They will not settle the mind.   [108]

The great teacher Śākyamuni Buddha has stated that one
must forget about those things which are known as the fourteen
hazy views about this world. The fourteen hazy views are:

a. Four that hold on to the past as one extreme:
   i. The self and the world are permanent,
   ii. The self and the world are non-permanent,
   iii. They are both [permanent and non-
        permanent],
   iv. They are neither [permanent nor non-
        permanent].
b. Four that hold on to the future as one extreme:
   i. The self and the world are eternal,
   ii. The self and the world are non-eternal,
   iii. They are both [eternal and non-eternal],
   iv. They are neither [eternal nor non-eternal].
c. Four that deal with Nirvāṇa:
   i. A Tathāgata will appear at the time of one's
      death,
   ii. A Tathāgata will not appear,
   iii. A Tathāgata will both appear and not appear,
   iv. A Tathāgata will neither appear nor not appear
       at the time of one's death.
d. Two which deal with the body and the life force:
   i. The body and the life force are one substance,
      and
   ii. The body and the life force are different
       substances.

[81] *See* Guenther & Kawamura, *Mind in Buddhist Psychology*, pp. 80–81;
and G. M. Nagao, "The Silence of the Buddha and its Mādhyamika Interpretation" in *Studies in Indology and Buddhalogy*, pp. 137–51.

With these views, the mind will not become settled; one's head will spin, and one's mind will get tired out.

Here, these views are spoken about as being 'hazy' because when heretics, who start out [from the premise] that the self is permanent, are asked about these topics, their replies are not clear, because they think that the premise 'a self does not exist' has nothing to do with hazy views, and that even the negation of a self is meaningless.

160 *An explanation of dependent origination which properly counteracts hazy views.*

This consists of two parts:

161. The subject matter of dependent origination,[82] and
162. A discussion of its depth.

161 *The subject matter of dependent origination.*

The Buddha has said, "From the loss of intrinsic awareness comes action;
From this, perception; from perception come name and patterns;
From these, the six bases of perception;
And from these come all forms of rapport.   [109]

Now then, how is dependent origination to be understood? ⟨53⟩ The Buddha has stated that from the loss of intrinsic awareness, which gives rise to a lack of understanding of the meaning of the fact that there is no abiding principle, there

---

[82] See Mi-pham's *mKhas-'jug*, fols. 17b–23a; N. Aiyaswami Sastri, *Ārya Śālistamba Sūtra*; Shoson Miyamoto, "A Re-appraisal of Pratītya-samutpāda," *Studies in Indology and Buddhalogy*, pp. 152–64; Steven D. Goodman, "Situational Patterning: *Pratītyasamutpāda*," *Crystal Mirror*, vol. 3. For a discussion on why the twelvefold chain of dependent origination begins with 'a loss of intrinsic awareness', *see* Guenther & Kawamura, *Mind in Buddhist Psychology*, p. xviii.

comes action, which is a driving force. From that [action] comes perception, which has a twofold function of being both a potential and that which gives direction to the potential. From this come 'concepts' which are classified under four heads— feelings, conceptualizations, and so on—and 'patterns', for example, an embryo. From these, come the six bases of perception (such as the eye) which are the internal fields. From these, come the six forms of rapport, which [may be defined as] the coming together of the sensory organ, a sensory object, and a perceptual operation.

> *From rapport come all feelings;*
> *With feeling as its foundation, craving arises;*
> *From craving arises appropriation; and from this,*
> *One's 'potential life-form'; from a potential life-form*
> *   arises birth.*   [110]

From rapport come all positive and negative feelings. With feelings as its foundation, craving, which is to take and reject, arises. From craving comes appropriation, which is to pursue [desired] things. From this arises 'potential life-form', which is a readiness to perform karmic activities. From a potential life-form comes a future birth.

> *When there is birth, frustrations such as misery,*
> *Sickness, old age, and the poverty that results*
> *From desires, death, fears and so on, increase.*
> *When birth no longer takes place, everything*
> *   comes to an end.*   [111]

When there is birth, frustrations such as misery, sickness, old age, and the poverty that results from desires, death, fears, lamentation, and unhappiness increase. When the loss of intrinsic awareness and all the other stages are overcome so that birth no longer takes place, all frustrations such as misery will come to an end.

162   A *discussion of its depth.*

> *This dependent origination is the precious and*
> *Profound treasure of the Buddha's teaching.*
> *Whosoever sees this as real,*
> *Realizes the Buddha and sees the Supreme*
> *Unity.*   [112]

This dependent origination which has been explained
above, is the great treasure of the Buddha's teaching and, from
among ⟨54⟩ the many topics, is the deepest and most precious
meaning, like a powerful wish-fulfilling gem. Whosoever truly
sees this dependent origination, sees the unity of Saṁsāra and
Nirvāṇa[83] and realizes, with the eyes of appreciative discrimination, the truth of the Buddha's authentic being.

163   *The path of developing the vision.*

> This consists of three parts:
>
> 164. An explanation that the eightfold noble path
>   constitutes the path of developing the vision,
> 165. An explanation of how this comes about, and
> 166. The advice that appreciative discrimination by
>   which one sees the four noble truths is the main
>   concern of the path.

164   *An explanation that the eightfold noble path*
      constitutes the path of developing the vision.

> *View, livelihood, effort, attentiveness, mental*
> *Integration, speech, action, and understanding—*
> *These, when proper, form the eight components of the*
> *path.*
> *Cultivate these so that you will attain peace.*   [113]

---

[83] *chos-sku*, lit. 'authentic being'. The unity of Saṁsāra and Nirvāṇa
(*chos* = *ngo-bo* = *stong-pa-nyid* and *sku* = *rang-bzhin* = *snang-ba*) is the unity
of the open dimension of being (*stong-pa-nyid*) which is not anything (*chos*)
other than itself (*ngo-bo*) and the specific existence (*sku*) which carries qualities (*snang-ba*) within itself (*rang-bzhin*).

Proper view, which is perfect understanding,[84] was present on the previous path of seeing; proper livelihood, which removes evil ways of living; proper effort, which is to habituate oneself to the path; proper attentiveness, which makes the mind stay with its objective reference; proper mental integration, which is to keep the mind in focus; proper speech, which functions to bring to others the meaning of what has been understood; proper action, which is pure, such as renouncing the act of killing because life is precious; and proper understanding, which gives rise to expressions which explain the meaning of life—these are the eight components of the noble path.

The path is 'noble' because, by means of it, what must be removed is removed, and freedom is realized. A proper view is the component which constitutes perfect understanding; proper understanding is the component which constitutes making others understand; ⟨55⟩ speech, actions, and livelihood are components which constitute inspiration in others; and the remaining three are components which constitute the removal of obscurations; thus they are called 'constituent components'. Cultivate these eight so that you will attain the peace of Nirvāṇa.

165   *An explanation of how this comes about.*

> *This life is 'a world of suffering', and*
> *It has, as its main cause, suffering.*
> *The abolition of this cause leads to liberation.*
> *The eightfold noble path is the path by which one*
> *attains liberation.*   [114]

---

[84] Proper intellectual understanding (*yongs-su gcod-pa*, lit. 'to cut up well') in a Buddhist context is a prerequisite for those who have not yet realized the 'fact' that both the concrete individual and the entities of reality are devoid of an abiding principle. However, no matter how deeply one may intellectually understand this so-called 'fact', it remains a logical fiction until one 'knows' it through direct experience.

This life is the reason for speaking of this world as the truth of suffering and, in setting up frustration—that which causes life to be what it is—is this world's powerful cause, continually producing the various potential life-forms. When frustrations and their causes are completely extinguished, there is freedom. The path by which freedom is attained is the noble path comprised of the eight constituent components.

166   *The advice that appreciative discrimination, by which one sees the four noble truths, is the main concern of the path.*

   You must always endeavor to see the four noble truths
   Which have been explained just now.   [*115a,b*]

You must always endeavor to cultivate the path in order to see the reality of the four noble truths which have just now been explained.

167   *The joy of taking to heart its significance.*

   This consists of three parts:
      168. Relief even if one has a lowly disposition,
      169. Relief even if one has had little experience, and
      170. Relief which is to extend one's capacity to the fullest.

168   *Relief even if one has a lowly disposition.*

   Even householders, on whose lap Fortune is residing,
   Can ford the river of emotions through
      knowledge.   [*115c,d*]

Why do you think, "I who am a householder cannot see the noble truth"? ⟨56⟩A householder, 'on whose lap Fortune is residing', may possess sons, a wife, and other valuables, but even he, without giving up his wealth, can ford the river of emotions by knowing what to accept and what to reject—but not otherwise.

> *Even those who have experienced the Dharma,*
> *Have not done so because they fell from heaven,*
> *Or because they emerged from the darkness of the earth,*
> *But they have done so because they had their individual*
>   *existences engulfed by emotions.*   [116]

Even those great Buddhas and Arhats who have come face to face with the supreme citadel of the teaching have not done so by falling sometimes from heaven like rain, or by emerging from the darkness of the earth like harvest crops. Even those noble people, at some previous time, had been individual beings who were dependent on their emotions or were under the influence of their emotions, and therefore they had their existence determined in Saṁsāra. Therefore, if you cultivate yourself on the path, even you can attain the same result as those noble people who have become liberated by overcoming emotions.

169   *Relief even if one has had little experience.*

> *What need is there for me to ask you, over and over*
>   *again, to overcome fear?*
> *The purpose of my counsel is exactly this:*
> *The Buddha has declared, "One must control*
>   *one's mind.*
> *The mind is the root of life's meaning."*   [117]

What need is there for me to ask you, over and over again, not to be afraid of assailants, by saying, "Be freed from fear of others." The essence of my advice is this: You must control your mind. Even the Buddha has declared, "The mind is the root of life's meaning. It is proper for one to control the mind, ⟨57⟩ because he who has controlled his mind is happy."

170 Relief which is to extend one's capacity to the
fullest.

**Any such counsel given to you would be difficult
Even for the ascetics to accomplish. However,
Make your life meaningful by relying on the merits
Derived from whichever counsel you adopt.** [118]

If whatever counsel given to you previously, Oh King, is
difficult to accomplish even for the great ascetics who have
given up their homes, what can be said of someone like you
who lives the life of a king! Yet, do what you can, and make your
life meaningful by relying on the merits which are contained in
whichever counsel you adopt.

C. SUMMARY: HOW [THIS INSTRUCTION]
    IS POSITIVE IN THE END.

This consists of two parts:
> 171. The advice which reveals how one is blessed with
>   the joy which results [from the foregoing], and
> 176. The advice which is contained in the summary of
>   the meaning of the path and its effect.

171 *The advice which reveals how one is blessed with
the joy which results [from the foregoing].*

This has two parts:
> 172. Dedication, and
> 173. Its effect.

172 *Dedication.*

**Rejoice in the positive qualities of all things, and make
A dedication of even the three which you have properly
    cultivated
In order to realize Buddhahood.** [119a,b,c]

By rejoicing in the positive qualities—whether they be satisfying or unsatisfying—of all noble things gained by others, dedicate even the three, which you have properly cultivated by means of the three acts [performed by body, speech, and mind], to others, so that others will attain the citadel of the Buddha. And then, to all beings, make available that which makes the Mahāyāna goal superior.

173   *Its effect.*

This consists of two parts:
174. The incidental goals of the path, and
175. The ultimate goal of Buddhahood.

174   *The incidental goals of the path.*

Then by these positive accumulations, you   [*119d*]

Will appear in the capacity of a yogin in the worlds
Of gods and men, after innumerable (re)births.
The noble Avalokiteśvara, through his practice of
Enduring many miseries of sentient beings,   [*120*]

After many (re)births, removed sickness, old age,
cupidity-attachment, and hatred.   [*121a*]

Thus, when you dedicate yourself properly ⟨58⟩ to the positive qualities of the three pure motives,[85] your positive accumulations will increase. When you are born into the worlds of gods and men, after innumerable (re)births, you will appear in the capacity of a yogin who cultivates all of the paths in the same way as the noble Avalokiteśvara who, through his practice, endured the miseries of sentient beings in Saṁsāra

---

[85] 'Pure motive' means that the receiver of any gift or worship, the act of giving, and the person who makes a gift must all be in a state of disinterestedness. *See* H. V. Guenther, *The Jewel Ornament of Liberation*, p. 110, n.22.

and, out of his compassion, was (re)born into the world, over and over again, and removed the evils of the world, such as sickness, old age, cupidity-attachment, and hatred.

175 *The ultimate goal of Buddhahood.*

And may your life of protecting the world be like that
Of Bhagavat Amitābha in the Buddha realm.   [121]

Finally, when you have nothing more to learn, may your life, as a protector of the world, be infinite like that of the Bhagavat Amitābha, who, all alone, continues [his meditative practices] in the Buddha fields, as long as sentient beings remain in Saṁsāra.

176 *The advice which is contained in the summary of*
the meaning of the path and its effect.

After spreading, throughout the heavens of gods and
   the earth of men,
The pure glory which results from appreciative
   discrimination, ethical behavior, and charity,
Then make men on earth and gods in heaven
Truly give up their obsession with beautiful
   maidens.   [122]

And then, after you attain the quality of the
   Victorious One,
Subdue the frailties, birth, and death of sentient beings
   who are powerless due to their emotions.
Then enter the citadel wherein, when even the name
'(re)birth' has been transcended,
One is not overpowered by dangers, and one is
   freed from fears.   [123]

The advice summarizing the path and its effect which has been explained above, is as follows: After you have fully disseminated, throughout the heavens of gods and the world of men, the pure and well-renowned glory which comes from appreciative discrimination, ethical behavior, and charity, ⟨59⟩ then be sure to make your mind calm [by protecting it] from those attachments with which both gods in heaven and men on earth are obsessed, both mentally and physically, because they take refuge in heavenly maidens. Then, subdue the frailties, birth, and death which sentient beings accumulate, because they are powerless due to their emotions and frustrations. After you attain, for the sake of others, the quality of the Victorious One, who in his physical form[86] has the auspicious marks and signs of an Enlightened Being and who has conquered emotions, then for your own sake, enter the supreme citadel of calm and of authentic being, which is not overpowered by such afflictions as death, where even the name 'birth', which is beyond the discursive thinking of worldly people, does not apply, and where there is no ageing because there is not the baneful influence of old age, and where there is nothing of disease, and so on.

May even the fish and frogs within your Empire be
   protected
By the spread of the ocean of the Buddha's intention,
Through the advice given by the spiritual teacher,
   Nāgārjuna, and
May it fulfill their wishes, like a cool mountain
   breeze.   [124]

IV. THE POSTSCRIPT

This consists of two parts:
         A. The author, and
         B. The translators.

---

[86] See *Mahāyānasūtrālaṁkāra*, IX, 60–66.

A. THE AUTHOR

The *Letter to a Friend*, composed by Ācārya Nāgārjuna, was written to a very dear friend [of the author], a king by the name of bDe-spyod.

B. THE TRANSLATORS

The great scholar of India, Sarvajñadeva, and the venerable translator, Ka-ba dpal-brtsegs[87] of Zhu-chen, made the final version in response to a request ⟨60⟩ during the early spread of Buddhism.

---

[87] Ka-ba dpal-brtsegs is one of Padmasambhava's twenty-five disciples. He was considered to be the reincarnation of an Indian Mahāpaṇḍita and was born in Pembo north of Lhasa. He studied under both Śāntarakṣita and Padmasambhava and translated many volumes included in the Tibetan Tripiṭaka. See *Crystal Mirror*, 1975, *4*, 59–60.

APPENDICES

LAMA MI-PHAM'S
TABLE OF CONTENTS

I. Title.

II. Translator's homage.

III. The body of the commentary.
This [the body] consists of three topics:

    A. Introduction: How [this instruction] is positive in the beginning.

    B. Content: How [this instruction] is positive in the middle.

    C. Summary: How [this instruction] is positive in the end.

  A. Introduction: How [this instruction] is positive in the beginning.
This consists of two parts:

    1. The exhortation to listen so as to make a start.

    2. The advice to listen because it is a means for overcoming contempt.

  2. has two parts:

    3. Laying aside one's contempt for the form in which the advice is written.

    4. Laying aside one's contempt for its content.

B. Content: How [this instruction] is positive in the middle.
   This comprises two parts:
   5. An explanation that confidence [in the Dharma]
   is at the basis of a path which supports
   [those who are on the path to] liberation
   and an existence freed from conflicting
   emotions.
  11. The nature of the path.
5. has two parts:
   6. A summary of the six objects of sustained
   attentiveness of a Buddha, which are the basis for
   making pure what must be purified.
   7. A detailed exposition of the last three objects of
   sustained attentiveness.
7. comprises three parts:
   8. The supernatural.
   9. Charity.
  10. Ethical behavior.
11. [The nature of the path] comprises three parts:
  12. A summary.
  13. A detailed explanation.
  167. The joy of taking to heart its significance.
13. comprises six topics:
  14. Liberality and generosity.
  15. Ethics and manners.
  20. Patience and tolerance.
  25. Strenuousness and perseverance.
  28. Meditation and concentration.
  68. Discernment and appreciation.
15. [Ethics and manners] has four parts:
  16. Ethics and manners which must be observed.
  17. Elimination of activities which are incompatible
   with ethics and manners.
  18. Cultivation of carefulness, which is compatible
   with them.
  19. An exposition, by examples, of the benefits of
   carefulness.

20. [Patience and tolerance] comprises four parts:
    21. The advice to overcome anger, the cause.
    22. The advice to overcome resentment, the outcome.
    23. The fact that a specific outcome results from a specific state of mind.
    24. The advice to refrain from harsh words which sustain the state of indignation.
25. [Strenuousness and perseverance] comprises two parts:
    26. The sites in which the foundation of strenuousness and perseverance can be found.
    27. The advice to strive assiduously for that which harmonizes with one's intention and that which can be brought about.
28. [Meditation and concentration] comprises three parts:
    29. Setting out.
    62. Content.
    63. What one must do afterwards.
29. has two parts:
    30. The removal of instabilities which are not conducive to meditation and concentration.
    61. Adopting the four immeasurable divine states of the mind which are conducive to meditation and concentration.
30. has four parts:
    31. Being transfixed by an object.
    40. Being transfixed by the eight worldly concerns.
    49. Being transfixed by possessions.
    55. Being transfixed by pleasures.
31. has two parts:
    32. Controlling the senses so as to control one's ideas.
    37. Removing attachments, because one has understood what things are.
32. has four parts:
    33. The advice to guard the senses against the desire for another man's wife.
    34. The advice to guard the senses against other desires.
    35. The confusion which results from not controlling the senses.
    36. Praise of one who is able to control his senses.

37. consists of two parts:
    38. Overcoming attachments by thoroughly understanding a woman's body which is the principal pleasure in the world of sensuous desires.
    39. Removing attachments by knowing how passion functions.
40. [Being transfixed by the eight worldly concerns] consists of two parts:
    41. Aids to overcoming the eight worldly concerns.
    44. That which is to be removed.
41. has two parts:
    42. Aids identified.
    43. An explanation of those defects and benefits whose presence and absence determine the efficacy of an aid.
44. consists of two parts:
    45. The eight worldly concerns identified.
    46. Advice on the removal of the resulting evil.
46. consists of two parts:
    47. The evil identified.
    48. The way to get rid of it.
49. [Being transfixed by possessions] has three parts:
    50. A general explanation distinguishing possessions to be rejected from those to be accepted.
    51. In particular, rejection of acts which give little contentment.
    52. Aids to rejecting.
52. has two parts:
    53. The benefits derived from the aids.
    54. The evil consequences of not using them.
55. [Being transfixed by pleasures] has three parts:
    56. Family atmosphere.
    59. Food.
    60. Rejection of attachment to sleep.
56. has two parts:
    57. That which must be rejected.
    58. That which must be accepted.
61. Adopting the four immeasurable divine states of the mind which are conducive to meditation and concentration.

62. Content [of meditation and concentration].
63. [What one must do afterwards] consists of two parts:
    64. In general: The advice to accept wholesome acts and to reject negative ones.
    67. Specifically: The method by which one removes hindrances to mental integration.
64. has two parts:
    65. An explanation that negative acts weigh one down while positive acts lift one up.
    66. The advice to produce strong positive antidotes to negative acts.
68. [Discernment and appreciation] comprises two parts:
    69. A synopsis: The essence of the path having five stages of which the first is interest.
    72. A detailed explanation: Appreciative discrimination which is closely linked to attentiveness.
69. has two parts:
    70. An explanation that interest and so on are to be adopted.
    71. The process by which ego-inflation is overcome with the help of aids which are adopted.
72. consists of two parts:
    73. An explanation that appreciative discrimination is the root of every proper existence, be it Saṁsāra or Nirvāṇa.
    76. An exposition of the path of appreciative discrimination.
73. has two parts:
    74. A proper understanding by worldly people which becomes the basis of both an elevated existence and liberation, and
    75. An understanding by which one properly overcomes worldly concerns and which functions as the basis for liberation.
76. consists of two parts:
    77. A specific explanation of an opinionated view which inflates one.
    80. The subject matter of the path.

77. has two parts:
  78. An analysis of the complete personality which is devoid of a principle to which it can be reduced.
  79. An investigation of the psychophysical constituents of the personality which are the basis for assuming that a self exists as an ontological and factual reality.
80. consists of three parts:
  81. Three things which are inconsistent with the path and limit everything.
  82. Assiduous striving, which is desirable.
  83. Training oneself to understand the essence of the path.
83. consists of two parts:
  84. A general explanation: The three trainings.
  85. A specific explanation: Training in appreciative discrimination.
85. comprises two parts:
  86. The way to remove defiling factors of instability.
  151. The way to a correct realization of the purifying process.
86. has two parts:
  87. The most appropriate action to reverse tendencies towards egocentricity in a mind involved with this life.
  103. The most appropriate action to reverse tendencies towards egocentricity in a mind involved with the infinite extent of Saṁsāra.
87. has two parts:
  88. A summary.
  89. A detailed explanation.
89. comprises two parts:
  90. Contemplation of the impermanence of life.
  95. Contemplation of the rare occurrence of the unique occasion and right juncture.
90. has four parts:
  91. Contemplation of impermanence by thinking about the uncertainty of the time of one's death.

92. Contemplation of impermanence by thinking about the fact that one is certainly going to die.
93. Contemplation of impermanence by thinking about other examples.
94. A summary of the outcome.
95. consists of three parts:
  96. General explanation: Preciousness of having become a human being.
  99. Specific explanation: Sites in which four opportune interactions take place which provide favorable conditions.
  102. Think about how to remove the eight obstacles to happiness, which create unfavorable conditions.
96. has two parts:
  97. Why birth as a human being is precious.
  98. Why performing an evil act in one's existence is something very bad.
99. consists of two parts:
  100. In general, an explanation of the four opportune interactions.
  101. In particular, an explanation of spiritual friends.
103. [The most appropriate action . . .] comprises two parts:
  104. A synopsis.
  105. A detailed explanation.
105. consists of two parts:
  106. Although everything seems as it should be, one cannot be certain.
  119. The wide and awesome extent of frustrations.
106. has two parts:
  107. The ways in which the mind is unstable.
  118. The advice to gain a positive attitude from knowing about this instability.
107. has four parts:
  108. Because there is no certainty about who are enemies and who are friends, the mind is unstable.
  109. Because there is nothing which can satisfy, the mind is unstable.
  110. Because of the uncertainty of the hereafter, the mind is unstable.
  111. Because of the uncertainty of high or low, the mind is unstable.

111. consists of six parts:
   112. One cannot trust anything in the whole universe.
   113. One cannot trust pleasant companions.
   114. One cannot trust pleasant situations.
   115. One cannot trust pleasant surroundings.
   116. One cannot trust anything pleasurable.
   117. One cannot trust an established status or sphere.
119. consists of two parts:
   120. One must know that Saṁsāra simply means being frustrated.
   148. The advice that one must make efforts to avert the possibility of (re)birth, by knowing Saṁsāra.
120. has five parts:
   121. Frustrations in hell.
   134. Frustrations in the realm of animals.
   137. Frustrations in the realm of spirits.
   144. Frustrations in the realm of gods.
   147. Frustrations in the realm of demigods.
121. has two parts:
   122. A presentation.
   123. An explanation.
123. consists of two parts:
   124. The advice to get to know frustrations.
   133. The advice to remove their cause.
124. has two parts:
   125. Frustrations.
   126. Reflection on how and where they come about.
126. consists of three parts:
   127. Reflection on the time during which pain comes about.
   128. Reflection on how intolerable pain is when it takes place.
   132. Reflection on the length of time one experiences pain.
128. consists of three parts:
   129. In general.
   130. In specific.
   131. An analogy.
134. [Frustrations in the realm of animals] consists of two parts:
   135. Frustrations in general.
   136. Distinct and separate frustrations.

137. [Frustrations in the realm of spirits] consists of two parts:
    138. A presentation.
    139. An explanation.
139. consists of two parts:
    140. Pain.
    143. Cause of pain.
140. consists of two parts:
    141. Actual pain.
    142. Length of time one experiences pain.
144. [Frustrations in the realm of gods] consists of two parts:
    145. A presentation.
    146. An explanation.
148. [The advice to make efforts . . .] consists of two parts:
    149. The reason one must change one's life.
    150. The advice that one must quickly change one's life, because of that reason.
151. [The proper way to attain liberation] has two parts:
    152. One must be confident of liberation, which is the goal.
    153. One must experience the truth of the path, which is the cause.
153. consists of two parts:
    154. The path of seeing.
    163. The path of developing the vision.
154. has two parts:
    155. An explanation that the way as such consists of the seven constituent members of enlightenment.
    156. Specifically, an explanation of the profound meditative practice of appreciative discrimination which is intimately related to calmness.
156. consists of two parts:
    157. A dictum.
    158. An explanation.
158. consists of two parts:
    159. An explanation of hazy views which render nonsensical that which must be cultivated.
    160. An explanation of dependent origination, which properly counteracts hazy views.

160. consists of two parts:
    161. The subject matter of dependent origination.
    162. A discussion of its depth.
163. [The path of developing the vision] consists of three parts:
    164. An explanation that the eightfold noble path constitutes the path of developing the vision.
    165. An explanation of how this comes about.
    166. The advice that appreciative discrimination, by which one sees the four noble truths, is the main concern of the path.
167. [The joy of taking to heart the significance of the five paths] consists of three parts:
    168. Relief even if one has a lowly disposition.
    169. Relief even if one has had little experience.
    170. Relief which is to extend one's capacity to the fullest.
  C. Summary: How [this instruction] is positive in the end. This consists of two parts:
    171. The advice which reveals how one is blessed with the joy which results [from the foregoing].
    176. The advice which is contained in the summary of the meaning of the path and its effect.
  171. has two parts:
    172. Dedication.
    173. Its effect.
  173. consists of two parts:
    174. The incidental goals of the path.
    175. The ultimate goal of Buddhahood.
IV. The postscript. This consists of two parts:
    A. The author.
    B. The translators.

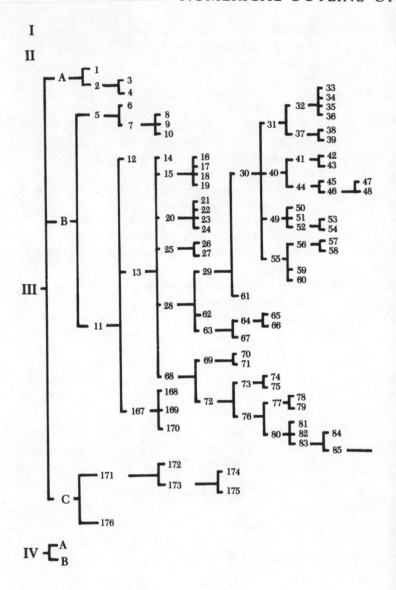

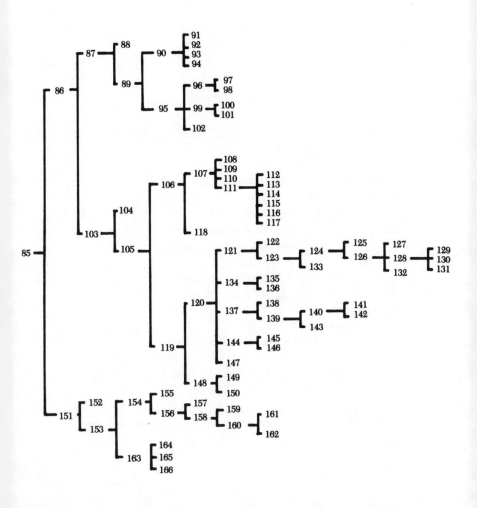

SA-SKYA PAṆḌITA'S
TABLE OF CONTENTS

Homage to Mañjuśrī Kumārabhūta

[Nāgārjuna's] "A Letter to a Friend" comprises three topics:
I. The setting out,
II. The content, and
III. What one must do afterwards.
I. The setting out.
   This consists of two parts:
      1. The reason for writing the letter, and
      2. The advice to take to heart its content.
   2. consists of two parts:
      3. That it is worthy of taking to heart, and
      4. The benefits derived from taking it to heart.
II. The content.
   This consists of two parts:
      5. A general explanation: The six objects of sustained attentiveness.
      12. A detailed explanation: The three trainings.

The system of enumeration used in this table of contents does not correspond with that used in the translation of Mi-pham's commentary.

5. has two parts:
    6. A general explanation, and
    7. Individual explanations.
7. has four parts:
    8. Charity,
    9. Ethical behavior,
    10. The Dharma, and
    11. The supernatural.
12. comprises three topics:
    13. Supreme ethical behavior,
    51. Supreme mental integration, and
    107. Supreme appreciative discrimination.
13. has two parts:
    14. The training which is conducive to an Arhat, and
    38. The training which is conducive to a householder.
14. has two parts:
    15. Accomplishing what must be learned, and
    26. Habituating oneself to aids to it.
15. has three parts:
    16. Training oneself in speech and bodily actions,
    17. Training one's mind, and
    21. An explanation of the two in general.
17. has three parts:
    18. Removal of emotions,
    19. Attainment of attentiveness, and
    20. Cultivation of patient acceptance.
21. has four parts:
    22. Training oneself by making an investigation of the mind,
    23. Training oneself by making an investigation of speech,
    24. Training oneself by making an investigation of the completed personality, and
    25. Training oneself by making an investigation of one's acts.
26. has two parts:
    27. Counteragents against emotions, and
    34. Counteragents against discursive thinking.

27. has three parts:
    28. Giving up that to which one is attached by thinking about it as one's mother,
    29. Giving it up by thinking about it as a defect and an evil reference, and
    30. Giving it up by thinking about other aspects.
30. has three parts:
    31. The fact that there is no abiding principle to which a thing can be reduced,
    32. The fact that nothing has an essence, and
    33. The fact that nothing can satisfy one.
34. has three parts:
    35. An investigation of compulsive performances, and then giving them up,
    36. The benefits derived from giving them up, and
    37. An investigation of the eight worldly concerns, and then giving them up.
38. has two parts:
    39. Do not perform evil acts for the sake of others, and
    42. Exert yourself in positive things which are wholesome.
39. has two parts:
    40. Do not perform evil acts, and
    41. It is proper not to perform evil acts.
42. has two parts:
    43. Actualizing causes which produce prosperity, and
    47. Acting in such a way that one does not produce attachments which hinder it.
43. has three parts:
    44. Attaining the seven precious jewels,
    45. Removing the six causes which produce evil existences, and
    46. Taking up only the jewel of a unique occasion and the right juncture.
47. has three parts:
    48. Do not relish overindulgence in sex,
    49. Do not relish overindulgence in food, and
    50. Do not relish overindulgence in sleep which makes one dull.

51. comprises two parts:
    52. Attain an elevated existence, and
    55. Gain liberation.
52. has two parts:
    53. Practice the four wholesome things, and
    54. Do not jeopardize one's practice by doing evil things.
55. has two parts:
    56. Give up things which are not conducive [to liberation], and
    57. Practice those things which aid it.
58. has two parts:
    59. Actualize counteragents against erroneous thinking, and
    70. Follow a proper path which produces counteragents.
59. has two parts:
    60. The significance of actualizing them, and
    61. How one goes about actualizing them.
61. has two parts:
    62. Actualizing counteragents, and
    63. Cultivating a proper view.
63. has two parts:
    64. The advice to cultivate a proper view, and
    65. The subject matter of a proper view.
65. has two parts:
    66. Gaining a proper view, and
    67. Removing others which are extreme views.
67. has two parts:
    68. Removing the six which are thought to be creative agents, and
    69. Removing the three which limit one.
70. has three parts:
    71. Put into practice the four truths,
    72. Put into practice the three trainings,
    73. Put into practice attentiveness which stays with the objective reference.
74. has two parts:
    75. Reflect on the status of frustrations, and
    102. The advice to become disgusted with Saṁsāra.

75. has three parts:
    76. Reflect on the impermanence of the world,
    80. Reflect on the difficulty of gaining the unique occasion and right juncture, and
    84. Reflect on frustrations.
76. has three parts:
    77. The impermanence of things,
    78. The giving up of extreme views, and
    79. A summary.
80. has three parts:
    81. The difficulty of gaining life,
    82. The attainment of a status of a yogin, and
    83. The giving up of the eight obstacles to happiness.
84. has two parts:
    85. A general explanation, and
    86. An explanation of each one.
86. has three parts:
    87. The misery of conditioned existence,
    91. The misery of change, and
    94. The misery of misery.
87. has three parts:
    88. There is no certainty,
    89. There is no satisfaction, and
    90. There is no end.
91. has two parts:
    92. How it comes about, and
    93. To exert oneself to positive qualities.
94. has two parts:
    95. Misery of an evil existence, and
    99. Misery of a heavenly existence.
95. has three parts:
    96. Beings in hell,
    97. Animals, and
    98. Spirits.
99. has two parts:
    100. Gods, and
    101. Demigods.
102. has two parts:
    103. The fruition as that which one attains, and
    104. The path as that which makes one attain the fruition.

104. has two parts:
    105. The explanation that the training is very precious, and
    106. The seven constituent members of enlightenment.
107. comprises three parts:
    108. The benefits derived from cultivating appreciative discrimination,
    109. Appreciative discrimination which is beneficial, and
    118. The advice to cultivate appreciative discrimination.
109. has two parts:
    110. The situation which results from not considering it, and
    111. The path which is to cultivate it.
111. has three parts:
    112. The twelvefold dependent origination,
    116. The eightfold noble path, and
    117. The four noble truths.
112. has three parts:
    113. The forward movement,
    114. The reversal,
    115. The benefits derived.
118. has two parts:
    119. The advice not to be lazy, and
    120. The advice to exert oneself mentally.
III. What one must do afterwards:
This comprises two parts:
    121. The counsel explaining how one must act, and
    126. The counsel that the outcome is determined by how one acts.
121. has two parts:
    122. The advice to make life meaningful by means of wholesome qualities, and
    123. The advice to make life wholesome by means of dedication.
123. has two parts:
    124. The advice to gain the physical marks and signs of the Victorious One, and
    125. The advice to attain the state of Being as such.

The Sa-skya Paṇḍita explained the summary of "A Letter to a Friend" in dPal-ldan.

LITERATURE
ON THE *SUHṚLLEKHA*

Of the many works attributed to Nāgārjuna, three have been classified under the category 'letter' (*spring-yig*).[1] The *bShes-pa'i spring-yig* (*Suhṛllekha*, "A Letter to a Friend") presents the chief principles of conduct for a householder.

Literature on the *Suhṛllekha* may be classified into the following five categories: verse text, commentaries, Chinese translations, translations into Western languages, and table of contents (*sa-bcad*).

Verse texts

The verse text of the *Suhṛllekha* has been translated from the text found in the *Tibetan Tripiṭaka, Peking Edition* (vol. 103, no. 5409). It was originally translated into Tibetan by Sarvajñadeva, to whom

---

[1] The three are: *rGyal-po-la gtam-bya-ba rin-po-che'i phreng-ba* (P. ed., vol. 129, no. 5658); *Srid-pa-las 'das-pa'i gtam* (P. ed., vol. 129, no. 5662); and

another verse text (vol. 129, no. 5682) is attributed. Both texts are essentially the same, except that text no. 5409 has one extra verse. Judging from the content of this verse (no. 124 in this translation), it is clear that it cannot be attributed to Nāgārjuna. If we should surmise that it was added by the translator, Sarvajñadeva, then we would have to question why text no. 5682 does not have the extra verse. Under the circumstances, we can conclude that it must have been added by a scribe at some later date. However, no Sanskrit version of either the verse text or commentaries on the *Suhṛllekha* has been discovered.

COMMENTARIES

Mahāmati's commentary, the *Vyaktapadāsuhṛllekhaṭīkā* (P. ed., vol. 129, no. 5690), is probably the oldest of the four commentaries which can be found at present and follows the traditional Indian style of commenting on the text word-for-word.[2] It is interesting to note the word *ṭīkā* in the title because this word usually designates a 'sub-commentary' implying that a *bhaṣya* (commentary) was extant. Could there have been such a *bhaṣya*?

The second commentary, written in 'interlinear style',[3] has been written by Mi-pham. It bears the title, *bShes-spring gi mchan-'grel padma dkar-po'i phreng-ba.*[4] Because Mi-pham was a most learned rNying-ma lama, one may conclude that his commentary represents a rNying-ma point of view.

The third commentary is that of a Sa-skya lama, Jetsun Rendawa.[5]

---

bShes-pa'i spring-yig (P. ed., vol. 103, no. 5409 and vol. 129, no. 5682).

[2] Th. Stcherbatsky calls this style "a philological interpretation" (see *Buddhist Logic,* vol. I, p. 40).

[3] 'Interlinear style' means that the words of Nāgārjuna's verses are incorporated into the sentences of the commentary.

[4] This text is found in *Jamgon Mipham's Shayting Chendrel Pema Karpo* and is a preliminary draft to Mi-pham's complete works which will appear in the *Ngagyur Nyingmay Sungrab Series,* edited by bSod-nam Kazi.

[5] According to Geshe Lobsang Tarchin, this commentary was published by the Tibetan Foundation Press, Darjeeling, 1960 (written in *dbu-med* script).

At present, the Geshe Lobsang Tarchin of Rashi Gempil Ling, New Jersey, is making a study and translation of it.

The last of the four extant commentaries was written by dGe-bshes bLo-bzang sbyin-pa.[6] This commentary is entitled *sLob-dpon klu-sgrub kyi bshes-pa'i springs-yig dang / de'i rnam-bshad dge-bshes blo-bzang sbyin-pas mdzad-pa bcas* (the colophon, however, gives *bShes-pa'i springs-yig gi rnam-bshad 'phags-pa'i dgongs-pa kun-gsal*) and comprises a table of contents, verse text,[7] and a commentary. bLo-bzang sbyin-pa composed this text in the solitude of dGa'-ldan chos-gling monastery.[8] That he was a dGe-lugs-pa may be inferred from his statement, "May this composition make it possible for the precious teachings of Tsong-kha-pa (Lord over the Dharma in the three levels of existence), [who expounded] the general and specific doctrine of the Buddha, to diffuse and spread for a long time."[9]

The *Suhṛllekha* has been considered an important text for all Buddhist schools in Tibet, evidenced by the numerous quotations to appear in various texts. For example, one can find many quotations in Ye-shes rgyal-mtshan's (1713–93) *Sems dang sems-byung gi tshul gsal-par ston-pa blo-gsal mgul-rgyan*,[10] which represents the dGe-lugs tradition, in sGam-po-pa's (1079–1153) *Dam-chos yid-bzhin gyi nor-*

---

[6] *Suhṛllekha by Ācārya Nāgārjuna*, edited by A. Sonam, Shastri, printed at The Pleasure of Elegant Sayings Press, Sarnath-Varanasi, 1971.

[7] The verses are numbered up to 122 due to the fact that verses 94 and 95 have both been numbered 94.

[8] *bLo-bzang sbyin-pas dben-gnas dga'-ldan chos-gling du bris pa . . .* (see p. 120). Mr. Lobsang Lhalungpa indicates that this was most probably Shangs-dga'-ldan chos-gling monastery, near bKra-shis lhun-po. From the preface (*sngon-brjod*) to his edition of the text, written by dGe-ming bsod-rnams, we learn that this text was originally brought from bKra-shis lhun-po to the Ladak Institute of Higher Education in Delhi where it was reproduced for use in the curriculum by dGe-bshes gnas-chung mchog-sprul thub-bstan dkon-mchog rin-po-che.

[9] *'dis kyang / rgyal bstan spyi dang khyad par / khams gsum chos kyi rgyal po tsong-kha-pa chen po'i bstan pa rin po che dar zhing rgyas la yun ring du gnas par byed nus par gyur cig* (see *bLo-bzang sbyin-pas*, p. 120).

[10] Yeshes rgyal-mtshan's text has been translated into English by H. V. Guenther & L. S. Kawamura and published as *Mind in Buddhist Psychology* (Emeryville, Cal.: Dharma Publishing, 1975).

bu thar-pa rin-po-che'i rgyan zhes-bya-ba theg-pa chen-po'i lam-rim gyi bshad-pa,[11] which represents the bKa'-gdams .tradition, and in A-'dzom-'brug-pa-'gre-'dud-dpa-'bo-rdo-rje's *kLong-chen snying-thig gi snyon-'gro'i khrid-yig thar-lam gsal-byed sgron-me* and 'Jigs-med-gling-pa's (1729–98) *Yon-tan rin-po-che mdzod,* which represent the rNying-ma tradition.

CHINESE TRANSLATIONS

The Chinese Buddhist tradition must have found this text of interest as it was translated into Chinese three times—by Guṇavarman, Saṅghavarman, and I-tsing.[12] Both Guṇavarman and Saṅghavarman made their translations during the Liu Sung period (420–77), and I-tsing during the T'ang period (618–905). It seems that the Chinese masters were not aware of Mahāmati's commentary, since it does not appear in the Chinese Tripiṭaka.

TRANSLATIONS INTO WESTERN LANGUAGES

Only the verse text has been translated into a modern language. These can be divided into translations from Tibetan and from Chinese. Translations by Robert Excell and Stephan Beyer into English,[13] and by Heinrich Wenzel into English and German,[14] are from the Tibetan verse text. S. Beal has made an English translation from Guṇavarman's Chinese translation.[15]

---

[11] sGam-po-pa's text has been translated by H. V. Guenther, *The Jewel Ornament of Liberation* (Berkeley: Shambhala, 1971).

[12] See *Hobogirin,* p. 99, and *Taisho Daizokyo,* vol. 32, nos. 1672–74.

[13] Robert Excell, et al., *The Wisdom Goes Beyond: An Anthology of Buddhist Texts,* pp. 15–44; Stephan Beyer, *The Buddhist Experience: Sources and Interpretations,* pp. 10–18.

[14] *Bçes pai phrin yig* ("Friendly Epistle"), in *JPTS,* 1886, pp. 1–32; *Brief des Nagarjuna an könig Udayana, Übersetzung aus dem Tibetischen,* Leipzig, 1886; see R. Yamada, *Bongobutten no Shobunken,* p. 123.

[15] See W. Winternitz, *History of Indian Literature,* vo. II, p. 347, no.3.

TABLE OF CONTENTS (*sa-bcad*)

Mi-pham, in making his commentary, has divided the text into various topics to form a table of contents. A translation of his table of contents and a corresponding numerical chart can be found in a preceding appendix.

Sa-skya Paṇḍita (Kun-dga' rgyal-mtshan) has written a table of contents which can be found in the *Sa-skya-pa bKa'-bum*.[16] A translation of his table of contents is included in the preceding appendix and a comparison of the two reveals that Mi-pham's table of contents is much more detailed than that of Sa-skya Paṇḍita.

bLo-bzang sbyin-pa's commentary also divides the work into various topics, providing an extensive and detailed analysis of the text. However, whereas Mi-pham emphasizes the six perfections (*pāramitā*), bLo-bzang sbyin-pa divides the text in accordance with the three kinds of beings (inferior, mediocre, superior) on the path to liberation.

From the content of Mi-pham's commentary which has been copied by 'Jam-dbyangs blo-gros rgya-mtsho, there seems to have been a separate text of Mi-pham's *sa-bcad* (table of contents).[17] This conclusion derives from the fact that a verse, which summarizes the reason Mi-pham wrote his commentary, is introduced by the phrase, "in the *sa-bcad*." The verse reads,

> The nectar, which removes the contagious diseases of this life
> And which is experienced as the sublime taste of calm,
> Unique to the hearts of those who have entered equanimity,
> Flows from the throat of this very sublime vessel.

---

[16] *Bibliotheca Tibetica, Complete Works of the Great Master of the Sa-skya Sect of Tibetan Buddhism*, vol. 5, pp. 446–47.

[17] The text reads: "This commentary, which has been written by Mi-pham 'Jam-dbyangs rnam-rgyal rgya-mtsho (who alone is the Lion's Roar in Tibet and who elucidates and systematizes Nāgārjuna's verses by incorporating the words of the verses into his commentary) has been copied by me, Ku-sā-li [i.e., one who eats, excretes, and sleeps] 'Jam-dbyangs blo-gros rgya-mtsho, in the hermitage of Yang-dben bde-mchog in the Zhe-chen monastery, in order to increase my positive qualities of good fortune."

That this nectar be implanted into my own mind and into the
   minds of others,
As the seed of a very pure and positive quality,
I have freshly composed this summary according to my own idea.
May its positive qualities be blessed by those who have attained
   Supreme Enlightenment.

TIBETAN LINE INDEX
TO NĀGĀRJUNA'S *SUHṚLLEKHA*

KA

kun gyi dge ba kun la yi rang zhing [*119 a*]

kun tu chog shes mdzod cig chog mkhyen na [*34 c*]

kun tu sbyor ba 'di gsum thar pa yi [*51 c*]

kla klor skye dang glen zhing lkugs pa nyid [*63 d*]

klu mchog rnams kyi mgo bo ji snyed pa [*35 c*]

bkres skom grang dro dal dang 'jigs pa yis [*91 c*]

bkrod pa gcig pa'i lam du nye bar bstan [*54 b*]

rkang pa'i reg pas nems par bde bzod pa [*71 a*]

skyabs med mgon med gnas med de slad du [*58 b*]

skyabs mdzad ri bsil bzhin du skongs par smon [*124 d*]

skye 'di sdug bsnal srid pa zhes bgyi ba [*114 a*]

skye ba dgra gyur pa bshes nyid dang [*66 b*]

skye ba 'gags pas 'di kun 'gag par 'gyur [*111 d*]

skye ba dpag tu med par lha mi yi [*120 a*]

skye ba zhes bgyi me khom skyon brgyad po [*64 b*]

skye ba yod na mya ngan na rga dang [*111 a*]

skye ba bzang po ma lags skye ba ni [*103 c*]

skye ba bzlong pa'i slad du 'bad par mdzod   [*64 d*]

skye bu rigs gzugs thos dang ldan rnams kyang   [*28 a*]

skye bo nyams thag mang po rjes bzung ste   [*120 d*]

skye bo'i rjes su 'brang ba'i khor ba pas   [*67 c*]

skyes pa bud med dag la stsol bar bgyid   [*11 d*]

skyes bu dam pa brten bgyi rgyal ba la   [*62 c*]

skyes bu dam pa la ni brten pa dang   [*61 b*]

bskyed pa shin tu mi bzad bsten 'tshal lo   [*91 d*]

bskyed pa'i sdug bsngal rgyun chags mi 'chos la   [*91 b*]

KHA

kha zas sman dang 'dra bar rig pa yis   [*38 a*]

kha cig kha ni khab gyi mig tsam la   [*92 a*]

kha cig lcags kyi mche ba ldan pa'i khyi   [*80 a*]

kha cig lcags kyi gsal shing rab 'bar ba   [*79 c*]

kha cig lcags las byas pa'i brangs chen du   [*82 c*]

kha cig til bzhin 'tshir te de bzhin gzhan   [*78 a*]

kha cig mdag me 'bar ba'i tshogs su ni   [*82 a*]

kha cig lpags rus lus shing gcer bu ste   [*93 a*]

kha cig mu tig bal dang rus pa dang   [*90 a*]

kha cig mtshan zhing kha nas 'bar ba ste   [*93 c*]

kha cig sog les 'gru ste de bzhin gzhan   [*78 c*]

kha cig srin bu sbur ba sna tshogs dang   [*81 a*]

khyod kyi khro ba'i go skabs dbye mi bgyi   [*15 b*]

khyod kyi thugs thul mdzod cig bcom ldan gyis   [*117 c*]

khyod gyi thugs su lta yang chud mod kyi   [*3 b*]

khyod gyis tshul khrims ma nyams mod mi dma'   [*7 a*]

khyod gyis bram ze dge slong lha dang ni   [*30 a*]

khyod la de skad gdams pa gang lags te   [*118 a*]

khyim thab brnyas bgyid jo mo lta bu dang   [*36 b*]

khrag sogs mi gtsang ba yang mi rnyed do   [*94 b*]

khrims ni rgyu dang mi rgyu'i sa bzhin du   [*7 c*]

khro ba spangs pas phyir mi ldog pa nyid   [*15 c*]

mkhas rnams dang po dpa' rab lags par 'tshal   [*24 d*]

'khon du 'dzin pas 'khrug long rnams skyed de　　[*16 c*]

'khon 'dzin rnam spangs bde bar gnyid kyis log　　[*16 d*]

'khor gyi slad du'ang sdig pa mi bgyi ste　　[*30 c*]

'khor ba chu shing snying po med pa la　　[*58 c*]

'khor ba dag na nges pa 'ga' ma mchis　　[*66 d*]

'khor ba dag tu yang bran nyid du 'gyur　　[*69 d*]

'khor ba de 'dra lags pas lha mi dang　　[*103 a*]

'khor ba'i btson rar 'jig rten 'di dag bcings　　[*23 d*]

'khor lo chen po bzhi ni khyod la mnga'　　[*61 d*]

'khor los sgyur ba nyid du gyur nas kyang　　[*69 c*]

'khrungs nas na rga 'dod chags zhe sdang rnams　　[*121 a*]

GA

gang gis 'di ni yang dag mthong ba des　　[*112 c*]

gang dag chos mngon bgyis pa de dag kyang　　[*116 a*]

gang dag dbang po drug yul rnams la ni　　[*24 a*]

gang zag log par lta bas legs spyad kyang　　[*47 c*]

gang la de gnyis yod pas srid pa yi　　[*107 c*]

gang la pha dang ma dag mchod pa yi　　[*9 a*]

gang zhig sngon chad bag med gyur pa las　　[*14 a*]

gang zhig mi ru skyes nas sdig pa dag　　[*60 c*]

gang zhig gser snod rin chen spras pa yis　　[*60 a*]

gar dang phreng ba'i khyad par rnam spong zhing　　[*10 d*]

gal te dge ba'i lhag ma 'ga' med na　　[*101 b*]

gal te mtho ris thar pa mngon bzhin na　　[*47 a*]

gus bas rtag tu bag dang bcas par mdzod　　[*13 d*]

go 'phangs mi rga mi 'chi bas mi 'tshal　　[*105 c*]

gong ma brnyes par ma gyur de lta na'ang　　[*40 c*]

gos la dri ma chags dang lus la ni　　[*99 c*]

grags pa nyams par 'gyur ba de drug spongs　　[*33 d*]

grong khyer gyi sgo 'gegs lags par mkhyen bgyi　　[*51 d*]

dga' dang shin tu spyangs dang ting 'dzin dang　　[*106 b*]

dga' po sor phreng mthong ldan bde byed bzhin　　[*14 d*]

dge dang mi dge rnam lnga chen po ste   [*42 c*]

dge ba'i las lam bcu po lus dang ni   [*5 a*]

dge ba'i rtsa ba yangs pas mkhyen par bgyi   [*43 d*]

dge ba'i bshes gnyen bsten pa tshangs par spyod   [*62 a*]

dge slong bram ze bkren dang bshes rnams la   [*6 b*]

dge bshes klu yis gdams pa'i char rgyun gyis   [*124 a*]

dgra bcom tshul khrims rjes su byed pa yi   [*11 a*]

bgyid pa de ni ches rab blun pa lags   [*60 d*]

bgyis pa ci 'dra'ang rung ste mkhas pas mchod   [*2 b*]

mgon po sku tshe dpag tu med par mdzod   [*121 d*]

mgo'am gos la glo bur me shor na   [*104 a*]

mgron dang yab yum dag dang btsun mo dang   [*30 b*]

rgod da 'gyod dang gnod sems rmugs pa dang   [*44 a*]

rgya mtsho gcig nas gnya' shing bu ga dang   [*59 a*]

rgya mtsho gnag rjes lta bur 'tshal bar bgyi   [*107 d*]

rgyan po 'byed dang 'dus la blta ba dang   [*33 a*]

rgyags phyir ma lags bsnyems pa'i phyir ma lags   [*38 c*]

rgyal ba'i bka' med pa dang mtha' 'khob tu   [*63 c*]

rgyal ba'i dbang pos kim pa'i 'bras 'drar gsungs   [*23 b*]

rgyal bas snying la 'bab dang bden pa dang   [*18 a*]

rgyal bas sangs rgyas chos dang dge 'dun dang   [*4 a*]

rgyal srid 'khor gyi nya sbal mang po dag   [*124 c*]

rgyun mi 'chad par rab bsregs kha yang bsgrad   [*82 b*]

sgrib pa lnga po de dag dge ba'i nor   [*44 c*]

sgrib pas bden pa mthong ba ma mchis so   [*102 d*]

brgya byin 'jig rten mchod 'os gyur nas ni   [*69 a*]

NGA

ngag dang yid kyis rtag tu bsten bgyi zhing   [*5 b*]

ngan skyugs 'phyag par bgyid pa de bas ni   [*60 b*]

mngon pa'i nga rgyal 'dod chags zhe sdang dang   [*12 b*]

lnga stong dag dang khrir yang 'chir mi 'gyur   [*96 d*]

sngon chad med pa'i rdul 'byung zhes bgyi ba   [*99 d*]

CA

ci nas de rdul tsam yang ma mchis pa   [88 c]
cig la cig za shin tu mi bzang pa   [89 d]
cung zad cig bsdebs khyod kyis gsan pa'i rigs   [1 d]
gcig pu zla ba nyi mas mi rtsi ba'i   [76 c]
bcing dang rdeg sogs sdug bsngal sna tshogs pa   [89 b]
lcags dang lcags kyu gdab pas btab te bkol   [90 d]

CHA

chang dang dus min zas la chags pa dang   [10 b]
chang dang mtshan mo rgyu ba ngan song ba   [33 c]
chang rnams las ldog de bzhin dge ba yi   [5 c]
chu yi chu bur bas kyang mi rtag na   [55 b]
chung du'ang rku ba chom rkun lta bu yi   [36 c]
chung ma gsum po 'di dag rnam par spangs   [36 d]
ches dkar nyid du ci ste mi bgyid lags   [3 d]
chos gzhan 'ga' yang mchis ma lags so   [27 d]
mchog ste chos 'dod rnams la tha ma lags   [17 d]
'chi ba zhi mdzad rgyal ba'i dbang po nyid brnyed nas   [123 b]
'chi ba'i dus la bab na sdig pa yi   [31 c]
'chi ba'i gnas su thub pas bka' stsal te   [13 b]
'chi 'pho'i sdug bsngal nyid ni de bas che   [98 b]

JA

ji ltar bde bshes sku gzugs shing las kyang   [2 a]
ji ltar mdzes can srin bus nyen pa na   [26 a]
ji srid mi dge de zad ma gyur pa   [87 c]
'jig rten kun gyi rnal 'byor dbang mdzad nas   [120 b]
'jig rten mkhyen pa rnyed dang ma rnyed dang   [29 a]
'jig rten las 'das ming tsam zhi la mi gYo ba   [123 c]
'jigs pa skyed par 'gyur na mi bzang pa'i   [84 c]
ljon shing 'bras bu med 'gyur 'di dag gis   [95 c]

NYA

nyi ma zla ba nyid thob rang lus kyi [*75 a*]

nyi ma'i gnyen gyis rab gsungs gang dag lags [*108 b*]

nyid kyi legs par spyod pa rnam gsum yang [*119 b*]

nyes par spyod pa'i las kyi zhags pa yi [*96 b*]

nyon mongs nyal thag sems can tshogs kyi 'jigs skye dang [*123 a*]

nyon mongs rag las so so'i skye bor bas [*116 d*]

gnyid dang 'dod la 'dun dang the tshom ste [*44 b*]

bsnyengs dang bral ba mang du gsol ci 'tshal [*117 a*]

TA

tā la'i yang tog bskams pa lta bu lags [*93 b*]

ting 'dzin shes rab chos mchog lnga nyid de [*45 b*]

gtum pos dbab cing lag pa gnab tu sgreng [*80 b*]

gter bzhin srog dang 'dra bar bsrung bgyi ste [*22 b*]

gtong dang tshul khrims lha rjes dran pa drug [*4 b*]

btang snyoms 'di bdun byang chub yan lag te [*106 c*]

btang snyoms rtag tu yang dag sgoms mdzod cig [*40 b*]

rtag tu mi brtan gYo dang gang dag cig [*24 b*]

rtag dang mngon par zhen dang gnyen po med [*42 a*]

rten cing 'brel bar 'byung 'di rgyal ba yi [*112 a*]

lto ba ri yi gtos tsam bkres pas nyen [*92 b*]

sta re mi bzang so rnon rnams kyis gshegs [*78 d*]

stan la mi dga' me tog phreng bsnyings dang [*99 b*]

stobs dbang zhes bgyi rtse mor gyur pa'ang lags [*45 d*]

brten nas rab tu mang pos zhi ba thob [*62 d*]

bltas pa tsam gyis klung yang bskam par 'gyur [*95 d*]

bstod smad ces bgyi 'jig rten chos brgyad po [*29 c*]

THA

tha mar mi gtsang snying po ma mchis pa [*56 b*]

thams cad rnam par smin pa mi bzad ldan [*47 d*]

thar pa bdag la rag las 'di la ni   [*52 a*]

thal ba yang ni lus par mi 'gyur na   [*57 c*]

thub pa chen po'i bka' ni snyan dgu zhing   [*3 a*]

thos dang tshul khrims bsam gtan ldan pa yi   [*52 c*]

mthun par gyur ba'i yul na gnas pa dang   [*61 a*]

mtho ris 'chi 'phro sbron bgyid 'chi ltas lnga   [*100 a*]

mtho ris na yang bde chen de dag gi   [*98 a*]

mtho ris bu mo'i nu ma rgyas pa la   [*70 a*]

mtho ris bu mos 'brangs zhing dga' ba dang   [*72 a*]

mthong bar bgyi slad rtag tu brtson par bgyi   [*115 b*]

'thob bgyid 'phags lam yan lag de brgyad lags   [*114 d*]

'thob bar 'gyur bar sangs rgyas zhal gyis bzhes   [*15 d*]

DA

dad dang brtson 'grus dag dang dran pa dang   [*45 a*]

dad dang tshul khrims gton dang thos pa ni   [*32 a*]

dam chos brjod la bsten slad smad mi bgyi   [*2 d*]

dam chos spyad pas de 'bras mchis par mdzod   [*59 d*]

dal gyis 'bab par lha yi bu mo ni   [*73 a*]

dud 'gro'i skye gnas na yang gsod pa dang   [*89 a*]

dus kyis bar du chod rnams dmyal ba yi   [*83 b*]

de ltar nyid kyi rtsal gyis 'bad par mdzod   [*88 d*]

de ltar 'di kun mi rtag bdag med de   [*58 a*]

de ltar sdug bsngal shin tu mi bzang lo   [*87 a*]

de ltar nongs par 'gyur 'tshal bsod nams ni   [*76 a*]

de ltar yang dang yang du sems pa ni   [*46 c*]

de ltar yi dwags rnams kyi sna tshogs pa'i   [*97 a*]

de ltar lags pas 'phags pa'i bden pa bzhi   [*115 a*]

de ltar bsams nas ya rabs rnams kyis ni   [*98 c*]

de ltas gang la yon tan 'di gnyis ldan   [*28 c*]

de dag dang bral khom pa rnyed nas ni   [*64 c*]

de dag rnams la bsam par mi bgyi ste   [*108 c*]

de dag spang bgyi de yi lcags sgog gis   [*23 c*]

de dag bzlog phyir bgyi ba btang nas kyang   [*104 b*]
de dag blo dang ldan na'ang 'gro ba yi   [*102 c*]
de dag la mchod grags par 'gyur ba dang   [*9 c*]
de dang 'dra bar yon tan ldan pa yi   [*27 c*]
de nas dge ba'i phung po 'di yis khyod   [*119 d*]
de nas dbang med dud 'gro yi dwags dang   [*101 c*]
de nang nyon mongs can la dang po ni   [*17 c*]
de ni bsgrims nas mngon par bsrung bgyi ste   [*54 c*]
de ni yon tan gzhan dang bral yang mchod   [*28 d*]
de bas khyod kyis dge chos spel slad du   [*13 c*]
de bas ches mchog dgos pa gzhan ma mchis   [*104 d*]
de bas ches mang nyid cig btung 'tshal lo   [*67 b*]
de bzhin bdag gi snyan ngag 'di ngan yang   [*2 c*]
de bzhin sdig pa'i las ni chung du yang   [*43 c*]
de bzhin sdug bsngal kun gyi nang na ni   [*85 c*]
de bzhin gzhan dag khro chu zhu ba yi   [*79 a*]
de bzhin shes rab gzhal med pha rol phyin   [*8 b*]
de yi rgyu ni skye bo 'jungs dga' ba   [*97 c*]
de yi gnyen po'i sgo nas rgyags mi 'gyur   [*46 d*]
de yi mod la mtshon bzhin mi gcod kyang   [*31 b*]
de yis blo 'di zhi bar bgyid ma lags   [*108 d*]
de las skye mched drug ste de las ni   [*109 c*]
de las dge ba spyod la brtson par bgyi   [*42 d*]
de las byung ba'i sdug bsngal de snyed do   [*35 d*]
de las srid pa srid las skye ba lags   [*110 d*]
de srid srog dang 'bral bar mi 'gyur ro   [*87 d*]
des ni dmyal ba'i sdug bsngal cung du la   [*86 c*]
des pa bdog mang ji ltar sdug bsngal ba   [*35 a*]
des pa 'dod pas phongs dang 'chi ba dang   [*65 a*]
don dam gzigs par bgyi slad dngos rnams la   [*27 a*]
dran dang bklags dang gzugs su bgyis rnams kyang   [*84 b*]
dran dang chos rab 'byed dang brtson 'grus dang   [*106 a*]
dran dang ting 'dzin ngag dang las mtha' dang   [*113 b*]

dran dang ldan par de dag bar du mnol   [39 d]

dran pa nyams pas chos kun 'jig par 'gyur   [54 d]

dran pa nye bar ma gzhag rnams kyis ni   [48 c]

dri nga ba dang sgo dgu dong pa dang   [25 b]

dri med ngo tsha shes dang khrel yod dang   [32 b]

gdug pa dug dang mtshon tsha dgra bo dang   [22 c]

gdong mdzes gser gyi padma ldan zhugs nas   [73 b]

bdag gi yid yul min par mgo snyoms mdzod   [29 d]

bdag nyid legs smon sngon yang bsod nams bgyid   [61 c]

bdag ni 'dis spyos 'dis btags pham par byas   [16 a]

bdag la gzugs mi gnas te de bzhin du   [49 c]

bde dags dga' ba nges par rab tu zhi mdzad de   [122 d]

bde dang mi bde snyan dang mi snyan dang   [29 b]

bde ba kun gyi nang nas srid zad pa   [85 a]

bde ba don du me la kun bsten kyang   [26 b]

bde ba'i bdag po bgyid pa ji lta bar   [85 b]

bde bar gshes pa'i gsung bsnyad las byung ba'i   [1 b]

bden pa rnam pa bzhi la 'bad pa mdzod   [52 d]

'dab mar ral gri 'dra tshal gnas rnams kyis   [72 c]

'di 'gog pa ni thar pa lags te de   [114 c]

'di ltar bzod mtshungs dka' thob ma mchis pas   [15 a]

'di dag rgyas mdzad srid pa'i rgya mtsho yi   [8 c]

'di na nyin gcig mdung thung sum brgya yis   [86 a]

'di ni de'i kun 'byung rgya chen te   [114 b]

'di ni zhi bar bgyi slad bsgom par bgyi   [113 d]

'di yi nyes pa shes kyang gsan par mdzod   [65 d]

'di yis bdag nor phrogs par gyur to zhes   [16 b]

'di la mngon brtson mdzad cig 'di dag ni   [45 c]

'di las gang zhig spyod pa'i ngo bo de'i   [118 c]

'dod chags zhe sdang med par bsten bgyi ste   [38 b]

'dod pa chung rnams de ltar ma lags te   [35 b]

'dod pa rnams ni phung khrol bskyed pa ste   [23 a]

'dod pa rnams la chags pa'ang mkhyen par mdzod   [26 d]

'dod pas phongs dang 'chi dang 'jigs sogs kyis   [*111 b*]
'dod spyod dga' dang bde dang sdug bsngal dag   [*41 a*]
rdo thal las bgyis dgung zla'i 'od kyis ni   [*3 c*]
sdig can dbug 'byung 'gags pa tsam zhag gi   [*83 a*]
sdig pa'i las rnams spyod pa 'ga' yang ni   [*31 a*]
sdug bsngal rgyun mi 'chad pa brten 'tshal lo   [*74 d*]
sdug bsngal phung po shin tu che 'byung ste   [*111 c*]
sdug bsngal gzhal yas thos nas rnams stong du   [*83 c*]
sdug bsngal ro gcig thob pa gang lags pa   [*97 b*]
sdug bsngal mi bzad phog snyam bgyid 'chal lo   [*71 d*]
bsdus 'joms du 'bod mnar med la sogs pa'i   [*77 c*]

NA

na rga 'chi sdug bral dang de bzhin du   [*46 a*]
na ba dang rga sogs sdug bsngal dum yi   [*65 b*]
na tshod mthun par ma dang bu mo dang   [*21 b*]
nor rnams kun gi nang na chog shes pa   [*34 a*]
nor mi bdog kyang yang dag 'byor ba lags   [*34 d*]
nor gzhan phal pa don ma mchis rtogs mdzod   [*32 d*]
gnas las babs pa ma lags lo tog bzhin   [*116 b*]
gnod pa du ma'i snod gyur lags mkhye mdzod   [*103 d*]
mnar med mi yi bud shing gyur pa yis   [*74 c*]
mnar med dmyal ba'i sdug bsngal rab mi bzang   [*85 d*]
mnal tshe'ang 'bras bu med par mi gyur par   [*39 c*]
rnam par 'jig dengs myags par 'gyur ba ste   [*56 c*]
rnam par spangs ba'i bsam gtan bzhi po yis   [*41 b*]
rnam par mdzes tshal sod pas rtsas nas slar   [*72 b*]
rnam smin nyams su myon na smos ci 'tshal   [*84 d*]
rnam shes de las ming dang gzugs rab byung   [*109 b*]
rnam gsum bka' stsal de las tha ma spang   [*18 d*]
rnam gsum mar me'i snang ba rab bzhes shig   [*76 b*]
snang nas snang ba'i mthar thug mun pa nas   [*19 a*]

PA

pang na dpal gnas khyim pa rnams kyis kyang   [*115 c*]
dpal la snang phyir yid kyi sdug bsngal che   [*102 b*]
lpags pas gYogs par rgyan yang logs shig gzigs   [*25 d*]
spyi'u tshug 'bras kyi cung 'phed bzhin du 'tshod   [*82 d*]

PHA

pha ni bu nyid ma ni chung ma nyid   [*66 a*]
pha rol phyin pa rgyal ba'i dbang po mdzod   [*8 d*]
phan pa'i gdams dag don po 'di lags te   [*117 b*]
phan tshun gdong du 'tshog cing mgren pa nas   [*94 c*]
phung po 'dod rgyal las min dus las min   [*50 a*]
phung po lhag ma bzhi yang stong rtogs bgyi   [*49 d*]
phyi nas bag dang ldan par gyur de yang   [*14 b*]
phyin ci log par lta dang the tshom ste   [*51 b*]
phyin ci log bzhir lta ba phung khrol ba   [*48 d*]
phye ma zhib mo bzhin du phye mar rlog   [*78 b*]
'phags pa spyan ras gzigs dbang spyod pa yis   [*120 c*]
'phrog pa'i chub rkun lags par mkhyen par mdzod   [*44 d*]

BA

bag yod bdun rtsi'i gnas te bag med pa   [*13 a*]
bar chad med par sdug bsngal rten gyur pa   [*96 a*]
bas par dge slong gyis gyang bgyi bar dga'   [*118 b*]
bud med gzhon nu'i lus ni logs shig tu   [*25 a*]
byams dang snying rjes dag dang dga' ba dang   [*40 a*]
bye ba phrag brgyar nyams su myong yang ni   [*87 b*]
lba ba byung ba smin pa'i rtag 'tshal lo   [*94 d*]
dbang gyur gang yin rigs kyi lha bzhin bkur   [*37 d*]
dbang thang che bas rgyags pa dgra bzhin gzigs   [*12 d*]
dbang phyogs las min rgyu med can min te   [*50 c*]
dbang phyogs lus gtogs dran pa bde gshegs kyis   [*54 a*]
dbang med gzhan dag lcags mchu rnon po dang   [*80 c*]

dbang med gzhan dag rdog pa lag pa dang   [*90 c*]
dbugs rngub dbugs 'byung gnyid kyis log pa las   [*55 c*]
'bar bas bsregs pa'i lus can 'di dag kyang   [*57 b*]
'byung gnas 'khor ba la ni skyo mdzad cing   [*65 c*]
'bras bu che lha rnams dang skal mnyam 'thob   [*41 d*]
sbyin dang tshul khrims bzod brtson bsam gtan dang   [*8 a*]
sbyin pa tshul bzhin stsal bgyi pha rol tu   [*6 c*]
sbyin las gzhan pa'i gnyen mchog ma mchis so   [*6 d*]
sbrang rtsi me tog mi gtsang lta bu'i tshig   [*18 c*]
sbron par byed pa'i 'chi ltas rnams dang 'dra   [*100 d*]

MA

ma 'des ma sbags pa dag bsten par mdzod   [*7 b*]
ma smin ma smin par snang smin la ni   [*20 c*]
ma bzhin phan par 'dod dang bran mo bzhin   [*37 c*]
ma yi thug mtha' rgya zhug tshig gu tsam   [*68 a*]
ma rig pa las las de de las ni   [*109 a*]
mal stan mtho la dga' dang glu dag dang   [*10 c*]
mi dge'i 'bras 'di rnams kyis sa bon ni   [*88 a*]
mi mchog khyod kyis thugs ni dbyung bar mdzod   [*58 d*]
mi rje rgyal po thugs kyi mtsho rgyas nas   [*124 b*]
mi bsnyengs nongs mi mnga' ba'i go 'phang brnyes par mdzod [*123 d*]
mi nyid ches thob dka' bas mi dbang gis   [*59 c*]
mi rtag bdag med mi gstang rig par bgyi   [*48 b*]
mi ni yang dag nyid du mi bde zhing   [*48 a*]
mi ni a mra'i 'bras bzhin ma smin la   [*20 a*]
mi gtsang gyi nar bor ba cung zad kyang   [*92 c*]
mi mtshang kun snod 'dra ba dgang dka' dang   [*25 c*]
mi mtshang nyid du'ang yang dag bsam par bgyi   [*21 d*]
mi 'jigs gang lags rdo rje'i rang bzhin no   [*83 d*]
mi shes las dang sred las byung rig mdzod   [*50 d*]
mun nag mtha' yas nang du 'jug 'tshal lo   [*76 d*]
mun nas snang ba'i mthar thug gang zag ni   [*19 c*]

mun pa'i mtha' dang snang nas mun mthar thug   [*19 b*]

me bzhin 'dod pa'i bde la yid byung mdzod   [*22 d*]

mya ngan 'das thob bgyid pa'i dge tshogs lags   [*106 d*]

mya ngan 'das zhi dul ba dri med pa'i   [*105 b*]

dmyal ba 'dud 'gro yi dwags rnams dag tu   [*103 b*]

dmyal ba rnams su rtag tu sdug bsngal gyur   [*77 d*]

dmyal ba bris pa mthong dang thos pa dang   [*84 a*]

dmyal ba'i rnam smin skal nod 'ga' ma mchis   [*30 d*]

dmyal bar 'thag gcod dbad pa'i 'khrul 'khor gyis   [*70 c*]

dmyal bar gnas pa gang yang rung bar gyur   [*101 d*]

smad rigs 'gas ni rnag dang phyi sa dang   [*94 a*]

smin pa dang 'dra smin la ma smin 'dra   [*20 b*]

smin par snang zhes bgyi ba 'drar rtogs mdzod   [*20 d*]

TSHA

tsha sgos bzod brlag chu tshan 'jug 'tshal lo   [*73 d*]

tshangs nyid chags bral bde ba thob nas slar   [*74 b*]

tshangs pa 'od gsal dag dang dge rgyas dang   [*41 c*]

tshangs pa'i 'jig rten bde ba thob par 'gyur   [*40 d*]

tshul khrims brtul zhugs mchog 'dzin rang lus la   [*51 a*]

tshul khrims dag dang shes rab bsam gtan gyis   [*105 a*]

tshul bzhin yid la bgyid pa de goms mdzod   [*27 b*]

tshe ni gnod mang rlung gis btab pa yi   [*55 a*]

tshe rings lha dang gang yang rung ba ni   [*64 a*]

tsher ma can la kun tu brgyud par bgyid   [*79 d*]

tshor ba'i gzhi las sred pa 'byung bar 'gyur   [*110 b*]

mtshag phyir ma lags lus gnas 'ba' zhig phyir   [*38 d*]

mtshan mo thun gyi stong smad bzlas nas ni   [*39 b*]

'tshal ba'i mthu dang ldan pa ma lags so   [*92 d*]

'tshe dang chom rkun 'khrig pa rdzun dang ni   [*10 a*]

'tsho ba la yang mngon par dbyes par mdzod   [*5 d*]

DZA

mdza' mo bzhin du snying la 'bab pa dang   [*37 d*]

ZHA

zhi 'gyur dge ba spangs pa rnams la ni   [*89 c*]

zhi bar ma 'gyur de nyid 'dra bar na   [*26 c*]

gzhan gyi chung ma mi blta mthong na yang   [*21 a*]

gzhan gyis grogs bgyir ci yang ma mchis kyis   [*52 b*]

bzhi ste de dag rnams kyi dang po mdzod   [*19 d*]

zhu ba 'bar ba 'khrigs pa ldud par bgyid   [*79 b*]

ZA

za bar bgyid cing 'dre ldgo smre sngag 'don   [*81 d*]

zad 'gyur mtho ris slad du sred mi bgyi   [*98 d*]

zas su 'bar ba'i khar 'bab bye ma 'tshal   [*93 d*]

gzugs dang mi ldan gzugs la bdag gnas min   [*49 b*]

gzugs ni bdag ma yin zhes gsungs te bdag   [*49 a*]

zla ba sprin bral lta bur rnam mdzes te   [*14 c*]

zla ba tsha ba dgun ni nyi ma'ang grang   [*95 b*]

bzlog pa nyid du mchis pas de slad du   [*66 c*]

'

'o ma 'thungs te da dung so so yi   [*67*]

'od kyis 'jig rten mtha' dag snang byas te   [*75 b*]

'od dpag med dang 'dra bar 'jig rten gyi   [*121 c*]

'ol yang mi bgyi char yang mi phod do   [*86 d*]

YA

yang dag rtog nyid lam gyi yan lag brgyad   [*13 c*]

yang dag lta dang 'tsho dang rtsol ba dang   [*113 a*]

yang dag lta la goms pa nyid du mdzod   [*47 b*]

yang song thig nag rab tu tsha ba dang   [*77 b*]

yang srid med par bgyi slad 'bad 'tshal te   [*104 c*]

yan lag brgyad po 'di dag dang ldan na   [*11 b*]

yi dwags nyid dang dmyal bar skye ba dang   [*63 b*]

yi dwags nang na'ang 'dod pas phongs pa yis   [*91 a*]

yi dwags rnams la sos ka'i dus su ni   [*95 a*]

yongs su rdzogs par thub pas gsungs de'i phyir   [*62 b*]
yon tan kun gyi gzhi rten lags par gsungs   [*7 d*]
yon tan bsten pas sku tshe don yod mdzod   [*118 d*]
yon tan gtso ldan gzhi las byung ba'i las   [*42 b*]
yon tan tshog kyi rjes su dran par bgyi   [*4 d*]
yon tan rang bzhin dge 'os bdag gis ni   [*1 a*]
gYul ngor dgra tshogs las rgyal de dag las   [*24 c*]
gYo ba'i sems ni thos mtshungs bu lta bar   [*22 a*]

RA

rang gi lag pa brgyang ba'ang mi mthong 'gyur   [*75 d*]
rang bzhin dgras 'brel gshed ma lta bu dang   [*36 a*]
rang bzhin las min ngo bo nyid las min   [*50 b*]
rab mchog lags par lha mi'i ston pas gsungs   [*34 b*]
rab tu bka' stsal de dag so so yi   [*4 c*]
rab tu drag btab bsdug bsngal gang lags pa   [*86 b*]
ri mor bris pa de 'drar rig par bgyi   [*17 b*]
ri lur bgrangs kyang sa yis lang mi 'gyur   [*68 d*]
rig pa kun tu 'byung bar thub pas gsungs   [*109 d*]
rigs dang gzugs dang thos pa lang tsho dang   [*12 c*]
rigs de tshangs bcas slob dpyon bcas pa lags   [*9 b*]
rigs pa'i bdag nyid nyin par mtha' dag dang   [*39 a*]
rus sbal phrad pa bas kyang dud 'gro las   [*59 b*]
re re'i bdag nyid rus pa'i phung po ni   [*68 a*]
re res rgya mtsho bzhi pas lhag pa yi   [*67 a*]
reg na mi bzang rma srol cher 'byin pas   [*81 c*]
reg pa las ni tshor ba kun 'byung ste   [*110 a*]
reg pa shin tu mi bzad bsten 'tshal lo   [*70 d*]
reg pa'i bde ba yun ring myong nas slar   [*70 b*]
ro bsgyur bgyid kyi gaṅgā'i klung min ltar   [*43 b*]

LA

las kyi 'bras bu gang la mngon par 'gyur   [*31 d*]
las kyis dbang gis phyir yang sa steng lhung   [*69 b*]

las ni bdag gir byas las ma 'das zhes   [*46 b*]
lan tshwa srang 'gas chu ni nyur du zhig   [*43 a*]
lung ma bstan bcu bzhi'i 'jig rten na   [*108 a*]
lus kyi kha dog mi sdug gyur pa dang   [*99 a*]
lus ngag yid kyi nyes spyad khyod kyis ni   [*88 b*]
lus mtha' thal ba mthar skam mthar 'drul zhing   [*56 a*]
le lo sdig pa'i grogs la brten pa dang   [*33 b*]
log par lta ba 'dzin dang dud 'gro nyid   [*63 a*]
log par smra ldan skyes bu rnams kyi ni   [*18 b*]
long spyod gYo ba snying po med mkhyen nas   [*6 a*]

SHA

sha dang pags pa'i ched du gsod par 'gyur   [*90 b*]
sha sbrang sbrang bu mchu rings khri phrag dag   [*81 b*]
shin tu nyams chung mi lta smos ci 'tshal   [*57 d*]
shes pas nyon mongs chu bo las brgal gyis   [*115 d*]
shes rab nor bdun lags par thub pas gsungs   [*32 c*]
shes rab med la bsam gtan yod min te   [*107 a*]
shes rab tshul khrims gtong byung grags chen dri ma med   [*122 a*]
shes rab tshul khrims bral ba bkur ma lags   [*28 b*]

SA

sa chu me rlung nyi zla bral thob mdzod   [*105 d*]
sa steng mi rnams 'chi bar 'gyur ba dag   [*100 c*]
sa dang lhun po rgya mtsho nyi ma bdun   [*57 a*]
sa rum nas mthon ma lags de dag sngon   [*116 c*]
sa la mi dang mtho ris lha ni na chung mchog   [*122 c*]
sangs rgyas nyid thob bgyi slad yongs bsngos nas   [*119 c*]
sangs rgyas de nyid rig pas rnam mchog mthong   [*112 d*]
sad khom gan lags de ni ngo mtshar che   [*55 d*]
sen mo mi bzang ldang pa'i khwa rnams 'thog   [*80 d*]
sems can nyes par spyad pa spyod rnams la   [*77 a*]
sems ni chu dang sa dang rdo ba la   [*17 a*]
sems ni chos kyi rtsa ba lags par gsungs   [*177 d*]

ser sna 'phags min lags par sangs rgyas gsungs   [97 *d*]

ser sna gYo sgyur chags dang snyoms las dang   [12 *a*]

so sor 'gyes chos can du mkhyen par mdzod   [56 *d*]

sra bas bcings pa'i lus can kha cig lo   [96 *c*]

sring mo lta bur rjes mthun gang yin dang   [37 *a*]

sring mo'i 'du shes bskyed bgyi chags gyur na   [21 *c*]

sred las len pa skye bar 'gyur ba ste   [110 *c*]

slad ma la yang mtho ris 'gyur ba lags   [9 *d*]

slar yang mun nag smag tu phyin gyur nas   [75 *c*]

slar yang me mur ro myags rgya ba yi   [71 *a*]

slar yang dmyal bar chu bo rab med pa   [73 *c*]

gsung gi mdzod kyi bces pa zab mo ste   [112 *b*]

gsum po 'di'i nang yang dag 'du bar 'gyur   [53 *d*]

gso spyod 'dod spyod lha lus yid 'ong ba   [11 *c*]

bsam gtan med par yang ni shes rab med   [107 *b*]

bsal te sangs rgyas zhing tu bcom ldan 'das   [121 *b*]

bsod nams 'dun slad 'phags pa'i dbyangs 'di dag   [1 *c*]

bslab pa brgya rtsa lnga bcu lhag cig kyang   [53 *c*]

HA

lha min dag na'ang rang bzhin gyis lha yi   [102 *a*]

lha yi 'jig rten dag nas 'phros pa la   [101 *a*]

lha yul nam mkha' dang ni sa steng rgyas mdzad nas   [122 *b*]

lha yul gnas pa'i lha rnams la 'byung ste   [100 *b*]

lha yul 'dod bde shin tu chen po dang   [74 *a*]

lhag pa'i tshul khrims lhag pa'i shes rab dang   [53 *a*]

lhag pa'i sems la rtag tu bslab par bgyi   [53 *b*]

lhun po mnyam pa snyid cig 'das gyur te   [68 *b*]

lhun po'i sbo la yun ring gnas nas ni   [71 *b*]

GLOSSARY
OF TIBETAN TERMS

KA

Ka-ba dpal-brtsegs, a famous translator, one of Padmasambhava's twenty-five disciples.

kimpa, *strychnos nuxvomica*, a poisonous cucumber.

kun-dga', Ānanda, a disciple of the Buddha.

kun-nas-nyon-mongs, defiling factors of instability.

kun-nas-slong-byed, gives rise to.

kun-'byung, cause of misery (see *'phags-pa'i bden bzhi-po*).

kun-sbyor, that which limits everything.

bka'-stsal, the Buddha has stated.

klad-kyi-don, introduction.

klu-sgrub, Nāgārjuna.

klu-mchog, eminent serpent.

skye-ba-gzhan, the next life.

skye-mched, bases of perception.

skyon, confusion.

This glossary was compiled so that the English translation of Mi-pham's commentary would not be 'cluttered up with foreign words'. It does not pretend to be exhaustive, as many more terms could have been added. Those terms and compounds which have been selected are either important or may not be found in dictionaries or other lexically-translated word lists, but will be useful to those studying the Tibetan language in conjunction with these texts.

KHA

kha-na-ma-tho-ba, objectionable.

khong-khro, anger.

khyab-pa, disseminate.

khyim-thab, family atmosphere.

khrel-yod, decorum (see *'phags-pa'i nor bdun*).

mkhyen-gnyis, two kinds of awareness: *ji-lta-ba-mkhyen-pa*, an awareness which sees reality as it is, and *ji-snyed-pa-mkhyen-pa*, an awareness of reality as it becomes manifest.

'khon-'dzin, resentment.

'khor-ba, Saṁsāra.

'khor-ba'i nyes-dmigs, the evils of Saṁsāra.

'khor-lo bzhi, four opportune interactions:
1. *mthun-par gyur-pa'i yul*, to dwell in a favorable place.
2. *dam-pa-la bsten-pa*, to associate with worthy people.
3. *legs-par smon-pa*, to practice true devotion.
4. *sngon-ma yang bsod-nams*, to possess good merits of previous lives.

'khor-lo'i sgyur-ba-nyid, universal monarch.

'khor-gsum, three pure motives:
1. *'khor-gsum-du rnam-par-mi-rtog-pa*, a pure motive without discursive thought.
2. *'khor-gsum-du rnam-par-rtog-pa*, a pure motive with discursive thought.
3. *'khor-gsum yongs-su-dag-pa*, a pure motive which is pure.

'khyal, idle talk.

GA

ga-ṅgā'i klung, Ganges river.

gang-zag, a concrete person, insofar as there is a becoming replenished (*gang*) and then a collapsing (*zag*).

go-skabs, opportunity.

gong-nas-gong-du, more and more.

goms-pa, to habituate oneself to something; to apply oneself.

dga'-ba, joy (see *byang-chub-kyi yan-lag bdun* and *tshad-med bzhi*).

dga'-bo, Ānanda, a disciple of the Buddha.

dge-'dun, Saṅgha. At the time of the historical Buddha, the Saṅgha comprised those who gathered to listen to him teaching. Later, the Saṅgha comprised those monks who had taken the precepts and who lived according to prescribed disciplinary rules. Of late, the Saṅgha comprises an individual or group intent on listening to the Dharma. See *rjes-su-dran-pa*.

dge-ba, wholesome; positive quality.

dge-ba'i grogs-po, a spiritual leader.

dge-ba'i phung-po, a positive accumulation.

dge-ba'i rtsa-ba, root of wholesome acts.

dge-ba'i bshes-gnyen, a spiritual friend.

dge-rgyas, Śubhakṛstna, name of a god.

dge-sems, a positive mind.

dge-slong, a monk.

dgra-bcom, an Arhat.

'gog-pa, the removal of misery (see *'phags-pa'i bden-bzhi-po*).

'gyur-phyag, translator's homage.

'gyod-pa, remorse.

'gro-ba'i sems-kyi tshul, function of the mind.

rgod-pa, overexuberance.

rgya-mtsho chen-po bzhi, four great oceans surrounding Mt. Sumeru.

rgyags-pa, vanity; ego inflation; egocentric thought; pride.

rgyal-ba, the Victorious One; the Buddha.

rgyal-ba'i bka'-med-pa ste sangs-rgyas ma-byon-pa dang byon-yang de'i bka' mi-thos-pa yul-mtha'-'khob-tu kla-klor skye-ba, to be born among the savages in a far off place when there is no Dharma, or to be born in a period when there is no Buddha (see *mi-khoms brgyad*).

rgyal-ba'i dbang-po, the Buddha.

rgyal-ba'i sangs-rgyas, the Buddha who is victorious (see *rjes-su-dran-pa*).

rgyas-bshad, a detailed explanation.

rgyud-la bsten-pa, foundation of life.

sgo-gsum, three gateways:
  1. *lus*, body,
  2. *ngag*, speech,
  3. *sems*, mind; thought.

brgya-byin, Indra, name of a god.
bsgom-lam, path of developing the vision.

NGA

ngag, speech (see *sgo-gsum*).
ngan-song, terrible existence; evil existence.
ngu-'bod, the Hell of Howling.
nges-par legs-pa, liberation; freedom.
ngo-tsha-shes-pa, self-respect (see *'phags-pa'i nor bdun*).
ngo-mtshar che-ba, a great miracle.
dngos-po, psychological reality; topics; things.
dngos-po'i gnas-tshul, things just as they are.
dngos-gzhi, content.
mngal-skyes, womb-born.
mngon-mtho, elevated existence.
mngon-du-bzhen-pa, earnestly wishing; an obsession.
mngon-pa'i-nga-rgyal, arrogance of showing off.
sngon-ma-yang-bsod-nams, to possess good merits of previous lives
     (see *'khor-lo bzhi*).
bsngo-ba, dedication.

CA

bcom-ldan-'das, Bhagavat; the Buddha.

CHA

chags-pa, attachment.
chu-bo rab-med-pa, Vaitaraṇi, a river in hell.
chog-shes-pa, contentment.
chos, Dharma (see *rjes-su-dran-pa*); life's meaning; entities of reality.
chos-kyi-sku, authentic being.
chos-mchog, highest worldly realization, the fourth level of the path of
     linking up.
mchod-par-'os, praiseworthy.
mchod-'os-su gyur-pa, to become well-renowned.
'chal-khrims, hypocrisy.
'chi-bar nges-pa, the certainty of death.

JA

ji-snyed-pa-mkhyen-pa, an awareness which sees reality as it becomes manifest (see *mkhyen-gynis*).

ji-lta-ba-mkhyen-pa, an awareness which sees reality as it is (see *mkhyen-gnyis*).

mjug-don, postscript; summary.

'jig-rten, the world; worldly.

'jig-rten-gyi-chos brgyad, eight worldly concerns:
1. *rnyed*, gain.
2. *ma-rnyed*, loss.
3. *bde*, pleasure.
4. *mi-bde*, pain.
5. *snyan*, kind words.
6. *mi-snyan*, abusive words.
7. *bstod*, praise.
8. *mi-bstod*, blame.

'jig-rten-gyi-mchod-'os, praiseworthy.

'jig-rten-pa'i yang-dag-pa'i-lta-ba, a correct world view.

'jigs-lta, opinionatedness about what is perishable.

rjes-kyi-bya-ba, what one must do afterwards.

rjes-su-mthun-pa, simpatico.

rjes-su-dran-pa, objects of sustained attentiveness:
1. *rgyal-ba'i sangs-rgyas*, a Buddha who is victorious.
2. *chos*, Dharma.
3. *dge-'dun*, Saṅgha.
4. *gtong-ba*, charity.
5. *tshul-khrims*, ethical behavior.
6. *lha*, the supernatural.

NYA

nyams-su-len-pa, to take to heart.

nyi-ma bdun, the seven suns which destroy everything at the time of *nam-zhig-bskal-ba* (*saṁvartakalpa*).

nyid-kyis, by oneself.

nye-'khor, neighboring hells in the four cardinal directions.

nyon-mongs-can-gyi-sems, an emotionally tainted mind.

nyon-mongs-pa'i kun-slong-ngan-pa, emotionally tainted attitudes.
gnyid, drowsiness.
gnyen-po, counteragents; a force which aids.
rnyed-pa, gain (see *'jig-rten-gyi-chos brgyad*).
snyan-pa, praise (see *'jig-rten-gyi-chos brgyad*).
snying-rje, loving-kindness (see *tshad-med bzhi*).
snying-po, intrinsic value.
snying-la 'bab-pa, to take to heart.
snyems-pa, mental inflation.
snyoms-las, laziness.

TA

ta-la, Tāla, a kind of palm tree.
ting-nge-'dzin, mental integration; meditative concentration; holistic
       experience (see *byang-chub-kyi yan-lag bdun*); meditative
       absorption (see *stobs lnga* and *dbang-po lnga*).
gtong-ba, charity (see *rjes-su-dran-pa* and *'phags-pa'i nor bdun*).
gtong-mi-'dod-pa, overconcern.
btang-snyoms, equanimity (see *byang-chub-kyi yan-lag bdun* and
       tshad-med bzhi).
rtag-pa, permanence (see *phyin-ci-log bzhi*).
rten-'brel, dependent origination.
rten-ma-ning, eunuchs.
rtogs-pa, to apprehend.
rtogs-zhig, gain an understanding (imperative).
stobs-lnga, the five unshakeable forces:
       1. *dad-pa*, confidence.
       2. *brtsom-'grus*, assiduous striving.
       3. *dran-pa*, sustained attentiveness.
       4. *ting-nge-'dzin*, meditative absorption.
       5. *shes-rab*, appreciative discrimination.
stong, the open dimension of reality; nothing in itself.
brtul-zhugs, a cult.
bstod-pa, praise (see *'jig-rten-gyi-chos brgyad*).

THA

thabs, most appropriate action; fitness of action.

thams-cad-mkhyen-pa'i-lha, Sarvajñadeva, a translator.

thar-pa, liberation; freedom.

thig-nag, the Hell of Black Thread.

thub-pa, the Buddha.

thub-gsung, the Buddha's teaching.

the-tshom-pa, indecision.

the-tshom-za-ba, to give way to indecision.

thos-pa, learning (see *'phags-pa'i nor bdun*).

mthar-thug, ultimate.

mthar-phyin, finally.

mthun-rkyen, that which is desirable; desirable (adj.).

mthun-par gyur-pa'i yul, to dwell in a favorable place (see *'khor-lo bzhi*).

mtho-ris, heaven; heavenly state; paradise.

mthong-ldan, Ajātaśatru.

mthong-lam, path of seeing.

DA

da-lta-nas, from now on.

dad-pa, confidence (see *stobs lnga*, *dbang-po lnga*, and *'phags-pa'i nor bdun*).

dam-chos, superior reality.

dam-pa-la bsten-pa, to associate with worthy people (see *'khor-lo bzhi*).

dam-pa'i chos, precious instruction.

dal-ba'i rten, a satisfactory unique juncture.

dal-'byor, unique occasion and right juncture.

dud-'gro, animals.

dud-'gro dang yi-dwags-nyid dang dmyal-bar skye-ba, to be born among the animals, spirits, or denizens of hell (see *mi-khoms brgyad*).

dul-ba, controlled (to see things but not to get involved).

dus-kyi dbang, the inexorable passage of time.

des-pa, My Lord (vocative).

don-gynis, two qualities:
1. *rang-don*, benefiting oneself.
2. *gzhan-don*, benefiting others.

don-mthun-du, common to . . . .

don-dam-gyi gnas-tshul, the absolute just as it is.

dran-nye, a short form for *Dam-pa'i chos dran-pa nye-bar bzhag-pa* (*Saddharmasmṛtyupasthānasūtra*).

dran-pa, to pay attention; attentiveness (see *byang-chub-kyi yan-lag bdun*); sustained attentiveness (see *stobs lnga* and *dbang-po lnga*).

drog-kyi skabs, stage of meditative heat (on the path of linking up).

bdag, Ātman; self; essence (see *phyin-ci-log bzhi*); an abiding principle through which something is what it is; philosophically, a reductionist idea or term.

bdag-med, the fact that there is no abiding principle to which a thing can be reduced.

bdag-yod, to have a primordial principle.

bdud-rtsi, immortality.

bde-ba, hedonistic delight; pleasure (see *'jig-rten-gyi-chos brgyad*); happiness (see *phyin-ci-log bzhi*).

bde-bar gshegs-pa, Sugata; Tathāgata.

bde-byed, Udayana.

bden-gnyis, two realities, usually referring to the conventional and the ultimate; in Mi-pham's commentary they refer to the truth of the extinction of frustration, and the truth of the path to the extinction of frustration.

mdor-bstan, a summary.

'du-byed, a motivating force; a driving force.

'du-shes, conceptualization; concepts; ideas.

'du-shes med-pa tshe-ring lha-nyid, to be born a long-living god who has no faculty for thinking (see *mi-khoms brgyad*).

'dun-pa, attachment.

'dod-rgyal, sheer imagination.

'dod-pa, passion.

'dod-pa'i-lha, Kāmadeva, name of god.

'dod-spyod-dga', sensuality; hedonistic delight.

'dod-yon, to hold on tenaciously.

'dod-log, sexual excess.

sdug-bsngal, frustration; misery (see *'phags-pa'i bden bzhi-po*).

bsdus-'joms, the Hell of Crushing.

NA

nang, Buddhist; a term used in distinction from *phyi*, outsiders, or non-Buddhists (see *phyi-rol-pa*).

nam-'chi-cha-med, time of one's death.

nam-'chi-ba'i dus, long night of death.

nam-zhig bskal-ba, *samvartakalpa*, the time when everything is destroyed by fire.

gnas-skabs, incidental.

gnod-pa'i-sems, vindictiveness.

gnod-sems, malice.

mnar-med, the Hell of Uninterrupted Pain; the Avīci hell.

rnam-byang, liberation, freedom.

rnam-gYeng, instabilities.

rnam-shes, perception; perceptual operation.

rnal-'byor-nyid, a yogin.

brnab-sems, selfishness.

PA

spyan-ras gzigs-dbang, Avalokiteśvara.

PHA

pha-ro-po, enemy.

phan-yon, benefits.

phar-rten, yonder basis.

phung-po, the psychophysical constituents of the personality.

phra-ma-tshig, slanderous words.

phyi, non-Buddhists.

phyin-ci-log bzhi, four opinionated views:
  1. *gtsang-ba*, purity.
  2. *bde-ba*, happiness.
  3. *rtag-pa*, permanence.
  4. *bdag*, essence.
phyi-rol-pa, heretics; outsiders, non-Buddhists.
'phags-pa'i bden bzhi-po, the four noble truths:
  1. *sdug-bsngal*, misery.
  2. *kun-'byung*, cause of misery.
  3. *'gog-pa*, the removal of misery.
  4. *lam*, the path.
'phags-pa'i-nor bdun, seven precious possessions:
  1. *dad-pa*, confidence.
  2. *tshul-khrims*, ethical behavior.
  3. *gtong-ba*, charity.
  4. *thos-pa*, learning.
  5. *ngo-tsha-shes-pa*, self-respect.
  6. *khrel-yod*, decorum.
  7. *shes-rab*, appreciative discrimination.
'phags-pa'i lam-gyi yan-lag brgyad, the eightfold noble path:
  1. *yang-dag-pa'i lta-ba*, proper view.
  2. *yang-dag-pa'i 'tshe-ba*, proper livelihood.
  3. *yang-dag-pa'i rtsol-ba*, proper effort.
  4. *yang-dag-pa'i dran-pa*, proper attentiveness.
  5. *yang-dag-pa'i ting-'dzin*, proper mental integration.
  6. *yang-dag-pa'i ngag*, proper speech.
  7. *yang-dag-pa'i las-kyi-mtha'*, proper action.
  8. *yang-dag-pa'i rtog-pa*, proper understanding.
'phen-pa, impelling force.

BA

bag-med, negligence.
bag-yod, carefulness.
byang-chub-kyi yan-lag bdun, the seven constituent members of enlightenment:

1. *dran-pa*, attentiveness.
2. *shes-rab*, appreciative discrimination.
3. *brtson-'grus*, energy.
4. *dga'-ba*, joy.
5. *shin-tu-sbyangs-pa*, alertness.
6. *ting-nge-'dzin*, holistic experience.
7. *btang-snyoms*, equanimity.

byang-sems, Bodhisattva.
byams-pa, benevolence (see *tshad-med bzhi*).
bying-ngas, fish.
bram-ze, Brahmin.
bla-na-med-pa, superior.
bla-ma 'jam-mgon, Guru Mañjuśrīnātha.
blo-ldog, reverse tendencies.
dbang-phyug, Iśvara, name of god.
dbang-po, sensory organ.
dbang-po lnga, five controlling powers:
1. *dad-pa*, confidence.
2. *brtson-'grus*, assiduous striving.
3. *dran-pa*, sustained attentiveness.
4. *ting-nge-'dzin*, meditative absorption.
5. *shes-rab*, appreciative discrimination.

dbugs-dbyung, relief.
dbugs-dbyung-pa, joy.
dbul-ba, poverty.
dbyangs-kyi yan-lag drug-cu, sixty modulations.
'bras-bu-che, Mahāphala, name of a god.
sbyin-pa, liberality and generosity.
sbyor-gyi las, acts which bind one to Saṁsāra.
sbyor-ba, setting out.
sbyor-lam, path of linking up; path of application.

MA

ma-nyams-pa, faultless.
ma-rnyed-pa, loss (see *'jig-rten-gyi-chos brgyad*).

ma-'dres-pa, mental clarity.

ma-byin-len, taking what is not given.

ma-sbags-pa, purity.

ma-yi thug-mtha', lineage of mothers.

ma-rig-pa, the loss of intrinsic awareness.

mang-du-thos-pa, learning.

mi-khoms brgyad, eight obstacles to happiness:

1. *log-par lta-ba 'dzin-pa.*
2., 3., 4. *dud-'gro dang yi-dwags-nyid dang dmyal-bar skye-ba.*
5., 6. *rgyal-ba'i bka' med-pa ste sangs-rgyas ma-byon-pa dang byon yang de'i bka' mi-thos-pa yul mtha'-'khob tu kla-klor skye-ba.*
7. *yul dbus-su skyes kyang yid dbang la skon zhugs glen zhing lkugs-pa nyid.*
8. *'du-shes med-pa ni tshe-ring lha-nyid.*

mi-snyan-pa, blame (see *'jig-rten-gyi-chos brgyad*).

mi-rtag-pa, impermanence; fleeting.

mi-brtan-pa, unsteady.

mi-mthun-pa, does not tally.

mi-bde-ba, pain, (see *'jig-rten-gyi-chos brgyad*).

mi-ldog-pa-nyid, a state in which one will not return to a previous one.

mi-gtsang-ba, an accumulation of filth.

mi-bzad-pa, excruciating.

mi-gsal-ba chos, dull and dim things.

mi-shes-pa, ignorance.

ming-gyis smos-pa, slanderous name-calling.

me-mur, the Hell of Fire Pit.

mod mi-dma', open-mindedness.

mya-ngan-las-'das, Nirvāṇa.

dmyal-ba, hell.

rmugs-pa, gloominess.

smad-pa, blame (see *'jig-rten-gyi-chos brgyad*).

TSA

gtsang-ba, purity (see *phyin-ci-log bzhi*).

rtsub-ngag, slander.

rtse-mo, culminating point.

brtson-'grus, strenuousness and perseverance; energy (see *byang-chub-kyi yan-lag bdun*); assiduous striving (see *stobs lnga* and *dbang-po lnga*).

tsha-dmyal, the Hell of Heat.

tshangs-pa, Brahmā, name of god.

tshangs-pa-nyid, Brahmāhood.

tshangs-pa'i 'jig-rten, a Brahmā world.

tshangs-par spyod-pa, Brahmacārya.

tshad-med bzhi, the four immeasurable divine states of the mind:

1. *byams-pa,* benevolence.
2. *snying-rje,* loving-kindness.
3. *dga'-ba,* joy.
4. *btang-snyoms,* equanimity.

tshig-rtsub, harsh words.

tshur-rten, hither basis.

tshul-khrims, ethical behavior (see *rjes-su-dran-pa* and *'phags-pa'i nor bdun*).

tshe-'di, this life.

tshor-ba, feelings.

mtshan-gyi-don, title.

mtshan-dpe, auspicious marks and signs of an enlightened being.

mtshan-gzhi, foundation.

mtshams-sbyor-ba'i dbang, the sustaining force of human embodiment.

DZA

mdzes-can, a leper.

ZHA

zhi, Nirvāṇa; inner calm.

zhe-sdang, hatred.

gzhan-gyis bsnyengs-pa, fear of others.

gzhan-don, benefiting others (see *don-gnyis*).

gzhal-yas-khang-pa, the abodes of gods.

gzhung-don, content; body of commentary.

gzhung-lugs, Buddha's teachings.

ZA

zag-bcas, anything which has the quality of falling apart; tainted by emotions.

gzugs, form; good looks.

gzugs-sku, physical form.

bzod-pa, patience and tolerance.

bzod-pa'i skabs, stage of patient acceptance (on the path of linking up).

'

'od-dpag-tu-med-pa, Amitābha.

'od-gsal, Prabhāsvara, name of a god.

YA

ya-rabs, supreme.

yang-dag-pa'i ngag, proper speech (see *'phags-pa'i lam-gyi yan-lag brgyad*).

yang-dag-pa'i ting-'dzin, proper mental integration (see *'phags-pa'i lam-gyi yan-lag brgyad*).

yang-dag-pa'i tog-pa, proper understanding (see *'phags-pa'i lam-gyi yan-lag brgyad*).

yang-dag-pa'i lta-ba, proper view (see *'phags-pa'i lam-gyi yan-lag brgyad*).

yang-dag-pa'i-dran-pa, proper attentiveness (see *'phags-pa'i lam-gyi-yan-lag brgyad*).

yang-dag-pa'i rtsol-ba, proper effort (see *'phags-pa'i lam-gyi yan-lag brgyad*).

yang-dag-pa'i 'tshe-ba, proper livelihood (see *'phags-pa'i lam-gyi yan-lag brgyad*).

yang-dag-pa'i las-kyi-mtha', proper action (see *'phags-pa'i lam-gyi yan-lag brgyad*).

yang-song, the Hell of Reviving.

yang-srid, possibility of (re)birth.

yi-dwags, spirits.

yi-rang-ba, joy.

yid-du-'ong-ba, pleasure; attractive.

yid-ma-'byung-ba, to caution one's mind by making it alert.

yid-mi-bde-ba, unhappy states.

yid yul-gyi dbang-du-ma-gyur-pa, not influenced as a result of following one's senses.

yul dbus-su skyes kyang yid dbang-la skyon zhugs glen zhing lkugs-pa nyid, even if a Buddha should appear, to be born a dumb person or a mute with physical defects (see *mi-khoms brgyad*).

ye-shes, knowledge.

yon-tan, virtue; precious; valuable; a person's spiritual growth; learning; a person of culture.

yon-tan-can, a worthy recipient.

gYeng-ba, transfixed.

gYo, dishonesty.

gYo-ba'i sems, scattered mind.

gYo-bar chos, fluctuating things.

RA

rang-gi-ngo-bo-nyid, pre-exist.

rang-gi-nyes-pa, one's shortcomings.

rang-gi-dbang-po, one's inner voice; a self-witness.

rang-don, benefiting oneself (see *don-gnyis*).

rang-lus phung-po lnga, the five psychophysical constituents which make up one's personality.

rang-bzhin-gyi-rgyu, self-realizing; self-actualizing.

rang-bzhin-gyi-gnas-skabs, one's own lifetime.

rab-tu-tsha-ba, the Hell of Intense Heat.

rig grol gnyis, to be freed from ignorance and to gain a state of awareness.

rigs, social status.

rigs-kyi-lha, family god.

reg-pa, rapport.

ro-myags, the Hell of Dirty Swamp.

ro-myong ba, enjoyable.

LA

lam, the path; the eightfold noble path (see *'phags-pa'i bden bzhi-po*).
lung-du-ma-bstan, hazy views.
lus, body (see *gso-gsum*).
lus-kyi-mtha', the inevitable end of the body.
lus-kyi srog-gcod, taking life.
lus-su gtogs-pa'i dran-pa, attentiveness to the body.
legs-par smon-pa, to practice true devotion (see *'khor-lo bzhi*).
len-pa, appropriation.
log-par lta-ba, wrong views.
log-par lta-ba 'dzin-pa, to entertain erroneous views (see *mi-khoms brgyad*).
logs zhig-tu blos gzhan, seen from a different point of view.
long-spyod, pleasures; the thing enjoyed.
longs-spyod, possession.

SHA

shin-tu sbyangs-pa, alertness (see *byang-chub gyi yan-lag bdun*).
shes-rab, discernment and appreciation; appreciative discrimination (see *byang-chub-gyi yan-lag bdun, 'phags-pa'i nor bdun, stobs lnga*, and *dbang-po lnga*).

SA

sems, mind (see *sgo-gsum*).
sems-can, human being.
sems dul-ba, to control one's mind.
sems-pa, to think; directionality of mind.
sems rtse-gcig-pa, a mind focused on its objective reference.
ser-sna, avarice.
so-sor 'gyes rang-ba'i chos-can, to have the nature of falling apart.
sor-phreng-can, Aṁgulimāla.
srid-rgyas-pa, the whole universe.
srid-pa, the possible existence; Saṁsāra.
sred-pa, craving.
slob-dpon, teacher.
gso-sbyor, the performance of purifying acts.

bsam-gtan, mental integration; meditation and concentration; meditative levels.

bsam-gtan bzhi-po, the four meditative levels.

bsod-nams-kyi snang-ba, the light of happiness.

bslab-gsum, the three trainings:

1. *lhag-pa'i tshul-khrims*, supreme ethical behavior.
2. *lhag-pa'i shes-rab*, supreme appreciative discrimination.
3. *lhag-pa'i sems*, supreme mentality.

HA

lha, gods; the supernatural (see *rjes-su-dran-pa*).

lha-min, demigods.

lha mi'i-ston-pa, the Buddha.

lhag-pa'i tshul-khrims, supreme ethical behavior (see *bslab gsum*).

lhag-pa'i shes-rab, supreme appreciative discrimination (see *bslab gsum*).

lhag-pa'i sems, supreme mentality (see *bslab gsum*).

lhun-grub, boundary situations; refers to emotions, death, life in a form of a living being, and over-evaluated ideas.

lhun-po, Mt. Sumeru.

A

a-mra'i 'bras, mango fruit.

BIBLIOGRAPHY

ABBREVIATIONS USED IN TEXT

Grub-mtha'   *Theg-pa mtha'-dag-gi don-gsal-bar byed-pa grub-mtha' rin-po-che'i mdzod*, by kLong-chen rab-'byams-pa.

mKhas-'jug   *mKhas-pa'i tshul-la 'jug-pa'i sgo zhes-bya-ba'i bstan-bcos*, by Mi-pham 'Jam-dbyangs rnam-rgyal rgya-mtsho.

Khrid-yig   *rDzogs-pa chen-po klong-chen snying-thig-gi sngon-'gro'i khrid-yig kun-bzang bla-ma'i zhal-lung*, by dPal-sprul O-rgyan 'Jigs-med chos-kyi dbang-po.

M.S.A.   *Mahāyānasūtrālaṁkāra*, ed. by Sylvain Lévi.

Mvyut.   *Mahāvyutpatti*, compiled by Sakaki, Ryosaburo.

P. ed.   *Tibetan Tripiṭaka, Peking Edition*, ed. by D. T. Suzuki.

PRIMARY AND SECONDARY SOURCES

Banerjee, Anukul Chandra. *Sarvāstivāda Literature*. Calcutta: Calcutta Oriental Press, 1957.

Beyer, Stephan. *The Buddhist Experience: Sources and Interpretations*. Encino, Cal.: Dickenson, 1974.

bSod-nams rgya-mtsho, *Bibliotheca Tibetica, The complete works of the Great Masters of the Sa-skya sect of Tibetan Buddhism*, 15 vols. Tokyo: Toyo Bunko, 1968.

Chattopadhyaya, D. *Tāranātha's History of Buddhism in India*. Simla: Indian Institute of Advanced Study, 1970.

dKon-mchog 'Jigs-med dbang-po. *Sa-lam-gyi rnam-bzhag theg-gsum mdzes-rgyan* [hand-copied manuscript (*dbu-can*), 22 folios].

dPal-sprul O-rgyan 'Jigs-med chos-kyi dbang-po. *rDzogs-pa chen-po klong-chen snying-thig-gi sngon-'gro'i khrid-yig kun-bzang bla-ma'i zhal-lung* [block print, 275 folios, no edition given].

dPal-sprul O-rgyan 'Jigs-med chos-kyi dbang-po. *Lam-nga rim-gyis bgrod-tshul dang sa-bcu'i yon-tan thob-tshul bye-brag-tu bshad-pa.*

Excell, Robert, et. al. *The Wisdom Goes Beyond, An Anthology of Buddhist Texts*. Bangkok: Social Science Association Press of Thailand, 1966.

Goodman, S. D. "Situational Patterning: *Pratītyasamutpāda*." *Crystal Mirror*, 3, 93–101. Emeryville, Cal.: Dharma Publishing, 1974.

Govinda, Lama Anagarika. *The Psychological Attitude of Early Buddhist Philosophy*. London: Rider, 1961.

Guenther, H. V. *Buddhist Philosophy in Theory and Practice*. Baltimore: Penguin, 1972.

Guenther, H. V. *The Jewel Ornament of Liberation*. Berkeley: Shambhala, 1971.

Guenther, H. V. *Kindly Bent to Ease Us*. Emeryville, Cal.: Dharma, 1975.

Guenther, H. V. *Philosophy and Psychology in the Abhidharma*. 2nd ed. Berkeley: Shambhala, 1974.

Guenther, H. V. *The Royal Song of Saraha*. Berkeley: Shambhala, 1973.

Guenther, H. V. *Treasures on the Tibetan Middle Way*. Berkeley: Shambhala, 1971.

Guenther, H. V. & Kawamura, L. S. *Mind in Buddhist Psychology*. Emeryville, Cal.: Dharma Publishing, 1975.

Kern, H. *Manual of Indian Buddhism*. Strassburg: Bombay Ed. Soc. Press, 1898.

kLong-chen rab-'byams-pa. *Theg-pa mtha'-dag-gi don-gsal-bar byed-pa grub-mtha' rin-po-che'i mdzod*. Gangtok, Sikkim: Published by Dodrup Chen Rinpoche, Saraswati Block Makers Lanka Varanasi-5.

Lamotte, Étienne. *La Somme du Grand Véhicule d'Asaṅga Mahāyānasaṃgraha)*. 3 vols. Louvain: 1938.

Lévi, Sylvain. *Mahāyānasūtrālaṁkāra*. Reprinted in Shanghai: 1940.

Lévi, Sylvain & Takakusu, J. *Hobogirin, Dictionnaire Encyclopédique du Bouddhisme d'après les sources Chinoise et Japanaises.* Fascicule Annexe. Tokyo: Maison Fransco-Japanaise, 1931.

Lin Li-Kouang. *Dharma-Samuccaya Compendium de la Loi* (2ᵉ Partie, VI–XII). Annales du Musée Guimet, Bibliothèque D'Études, vol. 74. Paris: Maisonneuve, 1969.

Mi-pham 'Jam-dbyangs rnam-rgyal rgya-mtsho. *mKhas-pa'i tshul-la'jug-pa'i sgo zhes-bya-ba'i bstan-bcos* [block print, 164 folios, no edition given].

Mitra, Ajay. *An Outline of Early Buddhism*. Varanasi: Indological Book·House, 1965.

Miyamoto, Shoson. "A Re-appraisal of *Pratītyasamutpāda*." *Studies in Indology and Buddhalogy*. Ed. Gadjin M. Nagao & Josho Nozawa. Hozokan, Kyoto: 1955.

Monier-Williams, Sir Monier. *A Sanskrit-English Dictionary*. London: Oxford University Press, 1970.

Nagao, G. M. "The Silence of the Buddha and its Mādhyamika Interpretation." *Studies in Indology and Buddhalogy*. Hozokan, Kyoto: 1955.

Nanjio, Bunyu. *The Laṅkāvatara Sūtra*. Kyoto: Otani Univ. Press, 1956.

Obermiller, E. *History of Buddhism (Chos-ḥbyung) by Bu-ston*. Heidelberg: O. Harrassowitz, 1931.

Pali Text Society. *Dīgha Nikāya*.

Pali Text Society. *Saṁyutta Nikāya*.

Poussin, Louis de la Vallée. *L'Abhidharmakośa de Vasubandhu*. 6 vols. Paris: Paul Geuthner; Louvain: J. B. Istas, 1923–31.

rJe-'ba'-ra-ba. *rJe-'ba'-ra-ba chen-po rgyal-mtshan dpal-bzang-gi bka'-bum*. 14 vols. Ngawang Gyaltsen & Ngawang Lungtok, ed. Dehradun: 1970.

rJe-'ba'-ra-ba. *Byang-chub sems-dpa'i bslad rin-po-che'i gter-mdzod-las / sa-lam drod rtags-kyi yon-tan skye-tshul bstan-pa*. Vol. 9 of rJe-'ba'-ra-ba's work.

Robinson, Richard. *Early Mādhyamika in India and China*. Madison: Univ. Wisconsin Press, 1967.

Roerich, G. N. (trans.). *The Blue Annals*. 2 vols. Calcutta, 1949, 1953.

Sakaki, Ryosaburo. *Mahavyutpatti*. Shingonshū Kyōto Daigaku, 1916.

Sastri, Aiyaswami N. *Ārya Śālistamba Sūtra*. Adyar Library Series, no. 76. Adyar Library, 1950.

Sastri, P. S. "Nāgārjuna and Āryadeva." *The Indian Historical Quarterly*, vol. 31, no. 3, 1955.

Schiefner, A. *Tāranātha de Doctrinae Buddhicae in India Propagatione*. Petropoli, 1868.

Smith, E. Gene. Introduction to *A Commentary on the Bodhicaryāvatāra* by 'Jam-mgon Mi-pham rgya-mtsho in *Ngagyur Nyingmay Sungrab*.

Sonam, A. *Suhrllekha by Acarya Nagarjuna* (A commentary on the Suhrllekha by Geshe bLo-zang sbyin-pa). Sarnath–Varanasi: The Pleasure of Elegant Sayings Printing Press, 1971.

Stcherbatsky, Th. *Buddhist Logic*. 2 vols. The Hague: Mouton & Co., 1958.

Stcherbatsky, Th. *The Conception of Buddhist Nirvāṇa*. The Hague: Mouton & Co., 1965.

Sthiramati. *Mahāyānasūtrālaṁkārabhāṣya*. *Tibetan Tripiṭaka, Peking Edition*. Ed. D. T. Suzuki. Tokyo-Kyoto, 1957.

Takakusu J. & Watanabe, K. *The Taishō Shinshu Daizōkyō*. Tokyo: Soc. for Publication of Taisho Tripiṭaka, 1960.

Tarthang Tulku. *Calm and Clear*. Emeryville, Cal.: Dharma Publishing, 1973.

Tarthang Tulku, ed. *Crystal Mirror, IV*. Emeryville, Cal.: Dharma Publishing, 1975.

Tibetan Tripiṭaka Research Institute. *Tibetan Tripitaka, Peking Edition*. Ed. D. T. Suzuki. Tokyo-Kyoto, 1957.

Winternitz, M. *A History of Indian Literature*. 3 vols. Univ. Calcutta, 1927.

Wylie, T. V. *The Geography of Tibet according to the 'Dzam-gling-rgyas-bshad*. Text and English translation, *Serie Orientale Roma, XXV*. Roma, 1962.

Yamada, R. *Bongobutten no Shobunken*. Kyoto: Heirakuji Shoten, 1959.

INDEX

TECHNICAL TERMS

Tibetan

sku, 85 n.83

'khor-ba mtha'-dag, 50 n.64
'khor-gsum, 13 n.24

gang-zag, 49 n.63
dge-ba'i chos bcu, 9 n.17
dge-tshul, 15 n.27
'gog, 9 n.15
sgo-gsum, 7 n.10

ngo-bo, 85 n.83
mngon-mtho, 9 n.18

chos, 9, 20, 49 n.63, 85 n.83
chos-sku, 85 n.83

ji-snyed-pa mkhyen-pa, 3 n.1
ji-lta-ba mkhyen-pa, 3 n.1
'jig-rten-chos-mchog, 41 n.50
'jig-rten-pa'i-lha, 34 n.44

lta-ba, 47 n.61
stong-pa-nyid, 85 n.83
stong-pa dang rten-'brel, 43 n.53

thabs, 13 n.23
mthar-thug, 31 n.43
mthong-lam, 41 n.51

don-gnyis, 5 n.4, 9 n.14
dran-pa, 41 n.48
drod, 41 n.50
bdag-med, 49 n.63
bdud, 8 n.12
'du-ma-byas, 16 n.30
'dod-chags, 16 n.29, 25 n.37
'dod-pa'i khams, 19 n.34

gnas-tshul, 28 n.40
snang-ba, 85 n.83
snang-tshul, 28 n.40

dpang-po, 9 n.17

pha-mes-gyi-lha, 34 n.44
phar-rten, 46 n.60
'phags-pa'i nor-bdun, 31 n.42

sbyor-lam, 41 n.50, 51

rtse-mo, 41 n.50

tshangs-par-spyod-pa, 55 n.70
tshur-rten, 46 n.60

gzhan-don, 9 n.14

zag-bcas, 16 n.30
bzod-pa, 41 n.50

yul, 16 n.30
yongs-su gcod-pa, 86 n.84
yon-tan, 9 n.16

rang-gi-dpang-po, 9 n.17
rang-don, 9 n.14
rang-bzhin, 85 n.83
rigs-gyi-lha, 34 n.44

lam, 9 n.15
las dang 'bras-bu, 43 n.52
lo-ka-chos-mchog, 41 n.50

bslab-pa'i gzhi, 15 n.27
bslabs-gsum, 49 n.62

lha'i-lo, 61 n.73
lhun-grub, 9 n.13

Sanskrit

upāsaka, 49 n.63
upāsikā, 49 n.63
kalpa, 53
paramārtha, 9 n.15
brahmacārya, 55 n.70
bhikṣu, 49 n.63
bhikṣunī, 18 n.32, 49 n.63

māra, 8 n.12
śikṣamānā, 49 n.63
śikṣapāda, 15 n.27
śramaṇera, 15 n.27, 49 n.63
śramaṇerika, 49 n.63
saṁvṛtti, 9 n.15

NAMES AND SUBJECTS

Abhidharma, 6
absolute, inherent character of, 28
absorption, meditative, 41, 79, 80
acceptance, patient, 19, 41
accumulations, healthy, 79f
act(s),
  of charity, 44
  five positive or negative, 39
  positive, 43, 44
    strength of, 39
    ten wholesome, 10
  pure, 55
  small offensive, 30
  unwholesome and evil, 39, 54
action, 30 n.41,.83f, 85, 86
  appropriate, 13, 57
  fitness of, 13
activities, three bodily, 10
Ajātaśatru, 18
alertness, 79, 80
Amitābha, 91
analysis, 37
Ānanda, 18, 56
anger, 19
Aṅgulimāla, 18
animals, 56
  frustrations of, 70f
application, path of, 41
  four parts of, 41
appreciation. *See* discernment,
  discrimination
appropriation, 84

arrogance,
  seven kinds of, 16
  of showing off, 16
Atīśa, 44
Ātman, 47
atmosphere, family, 33
attachment, 16, 25, 27 n.39, 40
  to ideologies, 47
  removing, 26f
  to sleep, 33, 35f
attentiveness, 40, 42, 79, 80
  to the body, 50f
  proper, 85, 86
  sustained, 35, 41
    six objects of, 8, 141
attitude, incorrect, 11
Avalokiteśvara, 90
avarice, 16, 74
awareness, intrinsic,
  loss of, 46, 47, 83, 84
  two kinds of, 3, 138

bDe-spyod, xv, 4, 93
behavior, ethical, 8, 9, 11, 12,
  24 n.35, 29, 31, 78, 91
  four qualities of, 12
  supreme, 49
being,
  authentic, 85
  human, 44f
    preciousness of, 53, 54
  sentient, 92

benevolence, 36
birth, 56, 59, 84
  eight situations of, 56
  five realms of, 77
body, 26f, 35, 82
  attentiveness to, 50
  nature of, 52
  of a woman, 26f
Brahmahood, 62
Brahman, 47
Buddha, xiii, 8, 9, 26, 55, 56
Buddhahood, goal of, 90

Calm, 37, 55, 80, 81
carefulness, 14, 17
  benefits of, 18
certainty, lack of, 58ff
charity, 8, 9, 11, 24 n.35, 31, 44, 91
clarity, mental, 11, 12
companions, pleasant, 61
concentration, meditative, 36ff, 48, 81. *See also* meditation
  three trainings of, 49
concepts, 84
conceptualization, 46
concerns,
  eight worldly, 28f, 141
  worldly, 44, 77
confidence, 7, 31
  as basis for the path, 41
  in liberation, 78
congregation, 9
constituents, psychophysical, 45, 46f, 48, 79. *See also* personality
contemplation, 24 n.35
  of impermanence, 51ff
contentment, 32
corporeity, and self, 45f
craving, 46, 47, 84
cupidity,
  -attachment, 16
  pleasures of, 24
Death,
  certainty of, 52
  five signs of, 75
  uncertainty of time of, 51

deceit, 16
decorum, 31
demigods, 64
  frustrations of, 76
desire, 70
  as cause of frustration, 73
  and guarding the senses, 24
Devadatta, 18, 46
devotion, 55
Dharma, 8
discernment and appreciation, 12, 13, 14, 40
discrimination, appreciative, 13, 29, 31, 40, 41, 42, 78, 80f, 85, 87, 91
  path of, 45ff
  supreme, 49
  training in, 48, 49
discursiveness, 37
disgust, with Saṁsāra, 53, 57
dishonesty, 16
drinks, intoxicating, 11
drowsiness, 40

Effort, proper, 85, 86
ego-inflation, 40, 42
egocentricity, action to reverse, 50
emotions, 88
enemies, 16
energy, 79, 80
enlightenment, seven members of, 79f, 146f
equanimity, 36, 37, 38, 79, 80, 81
essence, 45
ethics and manners, 12, 13, 14ff
  activities incompatible with, 16f
evil, removal of, 30
excess, sexual, 10
existence,
  elevated, 9
    basis for, 43
  human, 54
  root of every, 43

Faultlessness, 11, 12
feelings, 46, 84
food, 33, 34

forces,
  five unshakeable, 41, 142
  life, 82
  motivating, 46
freedom, 87
friends,
  Dharma, 56
  spiritual, 55, 56
frustration, 28, 48, 57, 65ff, 84, 87
  of animals, 64, 70f
  of demigods, 64
  as essential to liberation, 48
  of gods, 64, 74ff
  in hell, 64
  of spirits, 64, 71f
future, 82

Gain and loss, 29
gateways, three, 7, 65, 139
generosity, *See* liberality
giving, act of, 11
gloominess, 40
goal,
  incidental, 90
  ultimate, 90
gods, 36, 38
  death of, 75
  family, 34
  frustrations of, 74ff
growth, spiritual, 9

Happiness, 37, 45, 63
  eight obstacles to, 53, 56, 148
hatred, 16
heat, meditative, 41
hell,
  Avīci, 62, 69
  of Black Thread, 65, 66
  of Crushing, 65, 66
  of Dirty Swamp, 61
  of Fire Pit, 61
  frustrations in, 65ff
  of Howling, 65
  of Intense Heat, 65, 66, 67
  Neighboring, 67
  of Reviving, 65
  of Uninterrupted Pain, 65

hero, 26
hostility, 20
householder, 87f

Ideologies, attachment to, 47
immeasurables, four, 36, 149
impermanence, 28, 82
  contemplation of, 51ff
indecision, 40, 48
indecisiveness, 47, 48
indignation, 19
Indra, 60
inflation, ego-, 40, 42
insight, path of, 41
instability,
  of mind, 58ff
  removal of, 22ff, 37
instructions, baskets of, 6
integration, mental, 78
  five hindrances to, 40
  proper, 85, 86
interactions, four opportune, 53, 55, 138
interest, 40, 41
involvement, 9
Iśvara, 47

Jealousy, 76
joy, 36, 37, 79, 80, 89
juncture, right. *See* occasion, unique

Ka-ba dpal-brtsegs, 93
Karma, 60, 61, 67, 76, 78
Khri-srong lde'u-btsan, xiii
killing, 15, 70
Kimpa fruit, 25
Klu-sgrub, xii

Lamps, three, 24, 63, 64
laziness, 16
learning, 31
liberality and generosity, 12, 13, 14
liberation, 48, 86
  basis for, 43, 44
  confidence in, 78
life, 86f
  ethical, 15

-force, 82
-form, potential, 84, 87
impermanence of, 51ff
positive, 11
linking, path of, 41
livelihood, proper, 85, 86
living, six evil ways of, 32
loss. See *gain*
loving-kindness, 36
lying, 15, 70

Mādhyamika, xii, xiii
Mañjuśrī, xiv, 4
Mañjuśrīnātha, 3
manners. See *ethics*
meaning,
    life's, 88
    quest for life's, 20
meditation, 38 n.47
    and concentration, 12, 13, 14, 22, 36ff
    four levels of, 36ff
men, 22
    nature of, 44
mentality, supreme, 49
merits, 55, 89
mind, 20, 88
    emotionally tainted, 20
    four immeasurable divine states of, 22, 36, 149
    instability of, 58ff
    positive, 20
Mi-pham, xi, xiv f
motives, three pure, 13, 90, 138

Nāgārjuna, xi ff, 3, 93
Nāgas, xiii
names, and patterns, 83f
negligence, 17
Nirvāṇa, xii, 42, 43, 51, 71, 78, 80, 82, 85, 86
    two kinds of, 79

Objects,
    tainted perceptual, 16
    transfixed by, 23
obscurations, five, 40

obstacles, eight, to happiness, 53, 56, 148
occasion, unique, and right juncture, 51, 53ff
open-mindedness, 11, 12
operations, perceptual, 46
opinionatedness, 47, 48
opinions, erroneous, 44
organs, six sensory, 25, 26
origination, dependent, 81, 83f
overexuberance, 40

Padmasambhava, 93
pain, 72ff
    cause of, 74
    duration of, 68, 69f, 74
    Hell of Uninterrupted, 44
    intolerability of, 68f
    removing the cause of, 70
passion, 26, 27
past, 82
path, 40
    of accumulation, 9 n.16
    of application, 41
    of developing the vision, 77, 85ff
    eightfold noble, 85f, 146
    goals of, 90
    of insight or seeing, 41, 77
    linking, 41
    middle, xii
    nature of, 12
    six virtues of, 13ff
    subject matter of, 47
    summary of, 91f
    truth of, 78
patience and tolerance, 12, 13, 14, 19
peace, 85
people,
    ethical, 29
    four kinds of, 21f
    worldly, 29, 43
perception, 83f
    six bases of, 83f
perfections, six, 12, 13
permanence, 45, 82
perseverance. See *strenuousness*
person, praiseworthy, 29

personality,
    analysis of complete, 45f
    psychophysical constituents of,
        46f
perspective, wide, 81
pleasures,
    great, 62, 75
    and pain, 29
    transfixed by, 33
possessions,
    to be accepted, 31
    nature of, 11
    to be rejected, 31
    seven precious, 31, 146
    transfixed by, 31
powers, five controlling, 41, 147
praise and blame, 29
Prajñāpāramitā, xii
precepts, ten, 15
principle, lack of abiding, 28, 83
purity, 11, 12, 45

Qualities, two, 5, 144
quarrels, 20

Rapport, 83f
    six forms of, 84
realities, two, 9, 144
reality,
    investigation of, 79, 80
    knowledge of, 81
    open dimension of, 28
realization, highest, 41
realms, five, 64
    birth in, 56, 77
    frustrations in, 64ff
relief, three kinds of, 87
remorse, 40
renunciation, eight activities of, 15
resentment, 19, 20
Rong-zom chos-kyi bzang-po, 44

Saṁsāra, 42, 43, 47, 50, 58, 59,
        64, 85, 88
    disgust with, 53, 57
    natural state of, 77

Saṅgha, 8, 139
    seven classes of, 49
Śāntarakṣita, xiii, 93
Saraha, xiii
Sarvajñadeva, 93
seeing, 77. *See* insight
self,
    and corporeity, 45f
    and world, 82
self-respect, 31
self-witness, 9
senses, control of, 23ff
sex, improper, 15
sGrol mngon-pa, 44
situations,
    four boundary, 8
    pleasant, 61
sleep, attachment to, 35f
speech,
    four acts of, 10
    proper, 85, 86
    three kinds of, 20f
spirits, 56
    frustrations of, 64, 71f
Śrīmān, xiii
stealing, 15
strenuousness and perseverance, 12,
        13, 14, 21
striving, assiduous, 41, 47, 48
suffering, 86f
Sugata, 5, 7
Śūnyata, xii
supernatural, 8, 9, 10, 11
surroundings, pleasant, 62
Sūtra, 6

Tathāgata, 50, 82
teaching, 9
things, composite nature of, 37
thought,
    discursive, 13
    three acts of, 10
tolerance. *See* patience
trainings, three, 48, 49, 78, 153
trust, 60
truths, four noble, 9 n.15, 48, 87, 146

Udayana, 18
understanding,
    introspective, 37, 38
    proper, 43, 85, 86

Vaitaraṇī, 62, 66
vanity, 16
views,
    correct, 43
    erroneous, 43, 56
    four opinionated, 44, 45, 146
    fourteen hazy, 82f
    proper, 10, 85, 86

Vinaya, 6
vindictiveness, 40
vision, developing, path of, 77, 85ff

Wife,
    desire for another's, 23
    to be honored, 34
    three varieties to be rejected, 33f
words,
    kind and abusive, 29
    three kinds of, 20f
world, and self, 82